DEATH WINS ALL WARS

ALL WARS

DANIEL HOLLAND

SEE SHARP PRESS ◆ TUCSON, ARIZONA

For information contact:

See Sharp Press
P.O. Box 1731
Tucson, AZ 85702

www.seesharppress.com

Holland, Daniel.
   Death Wins All War / Daniel Holland ; Tucson, Ariz. : See Sharp Press, 2019.
   Includes bibliographical references and index.
   213 p. ; 23 cm.
   ISBN 978-1-947071-35-3

   1. Vietnamese Conflict, 1961–1975—Draft Resisters—United States.
   2. Vietnamese Conflict, 1961–1975—Protest Movements—United States.
   I. Title.

559.8

CONTENTS

Nothing will end war unless the people themselves refuse to go to war.

—Albert Einstein

The Specter of Death was the only protester left after the Minneapolis police dragged the rest of us out of the induction center at my sanctuary sit-in on June 18, 1969. Photo by Heine from the *Minneapolis Star-Tribune*. Courtesy of the Minnesota Historical Society.

PREFACE

Something dramatic happened almost every day in the Sixties. Whether it was on the news, in our personal lives, or on the street, change was in the air. It was up to us to create new ways to respond to civil rights, women's liberation, education, corporate America, drugs, sex, and rock & roll. But the Vietnam War overshadowed everything, and it was important to heighten public awareness of the antiwar movement and the ongoing catastrophe in Southeast Asia, so I put myself on the front lines of the antiwar campaign. Since the war ended, I have not led a public life.

As I present my story here, it is not my intent to write a history of the time but rather to let the lessons of history illuminate the evolution of my youthful naiveté into committed antiwar activism. I hope to explain how a young man came to the moral decision to engage in civil disobedience, and what compelled him to risk five years in prison. I'll do my best to explain the gravity of the situation for the individuals involved in draft resistance, and for the nation as a whole. This was a tumultuous time. Lives were lost. Souls were saved. It mattered where you stood.

The draft has been over for a long time, but young men are still required to register with Selective Service when they attain the age of eighteen, and it appears that women might be required to register at the same age. At present, there are actually some members of Congress proposing to reinstate the draft. I cannot stand by without speaking out publicly against this. I still maintain that conscription is antithetical to the very concept of a democratic republic that respects individual liberty. There is no way the United States government could have fought the war in Vietnam without the draft to feed coerced bodies into its war machine. If our government truly is "of the people, by the people, and for the people," then the government cannot force the people to fight a war they know is contrary to the best interests of themselves and their nation. Forced "service" of any kind isn't service, it's involuntary servitude.

When I first started to hear the crazy talk about re-instating the draft, I wanted to do my part to make sure we did not repeat the mistakes of Vietnam. As I contemplated my options, I came up with an idea of ordering the transcript of my 1969 trial for refusing induction, and to then present the trial as a play on the stage. The play would include a character called Me, which would be the present-day Daniel Holland, who would act as an Our Town-type of stage manager with the ability to stop the action on stage and comment on the situations or characters in the play. I decided to call the Daniel Holland of 1969 Danny, the name I answered to in those days. Danny defended himself in court and called as his witnesses Vietnam War veterans and other draft resisters to testify about how the draft and the war were devastating to all of us. There was also a fair amount of banter between the judge and Danny, some of it actually funny. Accordingly, it was not a typical trial, and I thought it would make an entertaining as well as an illuminating play.

I telephoned the clerk of the Minnesota district federal court and asked how I could obtain transcripts from a court case in 1969. The clerk informed me I could find those records at the US National Archives and Records in Chicago and provided me with the contact information. A very friendly woman there explained I could come to Chicago and make copies of the records myself, or her staff could make the copies and send them to me for eighty cents per page. I used a credit card to pay $113.60 for 142 pages of records. While I was waiting for my records to arrive, I started to organize an outline of the trial from memory and began to research how to write a play, which I had never done before. I could barely contain my excitement about the project and began pumping myself up to take on the role of Me myself, even though I had no professional acting experience. But I thought I would be perfect for the role.

Then the package from the National Archives arrived. There were a lot of pages to go through, so it took me a while to discover that the transcript of the actual trial, i.e., the testimony of witnesses and the opening statements and closing arguments by me and the assistant U. S attorney who prosecuted the case, were missing, replaced by a one-page handwritten synopsis:

"Mr. Holland opens and states case to the court and jury on his own behalf."

"Mr. Koenig sums up the case for the court and the jury on behalf of the Gov't."

The 142 pages were mostly pre-trial and post-trial motions, the judges jury instructions, and an appeal handled by an attorney on my behalf. I called my contact at the National Archives, and she explained very nicely this was standard procedure in court cases and was implemented to save space. Seriously? Forty pages of the record included an exact copy of the appeal filed in the George Crocker case. Simply replacing those pages with a 3 x 5 card with a handwritten note saying "See George Crocker appeal" would have saved enough space to preserve the content of my trial. It did me no good to tell her they destroyed the important pages of the historical record and saved the irrelevant ones. "I told you," she said, "you could come down here and copy the pages yourself. Then you would know what you were getting before you paid for them."

I won't say I fell into a deep depression, but my mood definitely dampened. My stepson, Noah Tabakin, and my wife, Gini Holland, have always encouraged me to tell my story of resistance. Now they sat me down and convinced me it was not the play itself that was important but the message it conveyed, and I would still have to tell my story even if I had to rely on my memory rather than a transcript. Of course, they were right, so I hereby maintain they are responsible for the book you are holding in your hands. Another culprit would be my good friend Paul Caster. Paul teaches drawing and video at an accredited art institute, and I approached him with the idea of a video documentary. Following a very engaging meeting, Paul requested an outline. When I presented him the list of topics I intended to cover, his response was, "You should write a book." OK then.

So, the chain of events I will present here comes directly from my memory of those years, but also the memories of friends and other participants in the anti-war movement, as well as newspaper articles and photographs, court records, FBI files, books, magazine articles, internet postings, and letters both to and from me. Many memoirs come with a caveat about the fallibility of memory, and there's been much research in the fields of medicine and psychology about its shortcomings. A rehash of the topic is not necessary here. As I write this preface, however, I must mention the February 2014 issue of *Scientific American*, which has an article about people with "highly superior autobiographical memory" (HSAM). I do not claim to have HSAM abilities, but I do have extensive background material to support, enhance, and refresh my memories, so am confident in the facts as presented.

Finally, I have a note on the use of names. If your name appeared in the newspaper or in the court records, if you signed a public statement or made public speeches, if you were an officer of the court or another public official, or if you were a recognized leader in the draft resistance or any of the several other antiwar organizations, you are already part of the historical record, and I used your real name in this book. If you were a friend or acquaintance of mine and your path peripherally crossed mine at the time, but I have been unable to contact you prior to publication, then I used just your first name. Nobody will know it's you unless you tell them. If you are in the first-name-only category and I felt something might be painful or embarrassing for you, I made up a new first name. Of course, I do not say anything I know to be untrue about anyone. The events I am relating in this memoir really happened.

That's my story, and I'm sticking to it.

* * *

The fog and the folly of war are well documented throughout recorded history. My coming of age story is inescapably linked to the body count, particularly of the American soldiers of my generation, but I cannot erase from memory the millions more who died. For what? The following list of dead of necessity is made from estimates as the hell that is war does not easily lend itself to the neatness of accounting, although the American deaths are extremely accurate, and the count was a regular feature of the nightly news. This is why I had to act in the Sixties, and why I must tell this story now.

3,000,000	Vietnamese civilians dead
1,100,000	North Vietnamese and Viet Cong soldiers dead
250,000	South Vietnamese soldiers dead
58,000	American soldiers dead (including MIA)
5,000	U.S. allied soldiers dead (South Korea, the Philippines, Australia, Thailand)
273,000	Cambodians dead
115,000	Laotians dead
92,000	French (and French colonial) soldiers dead
500,000	Vietnamese military and civilian dead (during French Indochina War)
60,000	Civilians, mostly children, killed by unexploded ordnance since the war ended
200,000	Vietnam Veterans suicides since the war ended
5,653,000	DEAD

1

TERRORISTS WITH TOMMY GUNS

July 10, 1959
Four Dead

Sitting in my father's lap while he read the evening paper to me is one of my fondest early memories. I loved how he could tell me what was going on in the world without our leaving the comfort of his overstuffed easy chair. Yes, I especially loved the funnies, but I was completely captivated by the news stories as well because my father would read them with such enthusiasm and animation in his voice the characters in the stories came alive for me. Consequently, I became an avid newspaper reader myself by the age of ten. Back in those days we received two newspapers per day, the morning paper waiting on the front step when we woke up, and the evening paper delivered just before supper. I devoured both of them.

I remember reading an article on page 3 of the July 10, 1959 *Minneapolis Tribune* headlined "Two Americans killed in South Viet Nam." Snipers, or "Terrorists with tommy guns," as the Associated Press reported it, shot two U. S. soldiers, Army Major Dale R. Buis and Master Sergeant Chester R. Ovnand, acting as military advisors in Bien Hoa, Vietnam, as they watched a movie in the mess tent on July 8. (It took two days for this news to filter down to our newspaper.) I was dumbfounded. I thought our country was at peace. I was, at the time, a naïve ten-year-old boy living in a small town in Minnesota. I took the paper to my father.

"Dad," I said, "why are they killing American soldiers in a country I never even heard of?" and I pointed to the article. He quickly read the piece. I swear on any and every thing that may be holy, my father then said, "It's not our fight. We should get our troops out of there." It was at this moment that the anti-war movement started for me. My dad was a pretty smart guy.

It turns out there were only about 700 U.S. troops in South Vietnam in 1959. Now two of those soldiers were dead. I couldn't believe it. I thought about their families, wondered if they had kids, wives, parents, and how difficult it must be for them. It would be many years before I learned there were two American deaths in Vietnam prior to this date. On June 8, 1956, Richard B. Fitzgibbon, Air Force, TSGT, was the victim of a homicide perpetrated by one of his own men. (His son, Richard B. Fitzgibbon III, LCPL, Marine Corps, would die in combat on September 7, 1965.) Harry G. Cramer, Captain, Army, died during a training action accident on October 21, 1957. James T. Davis, SP4-E4, Army, was the war's first battlefield fatality on December 22, 1961.

My father would die in a car accident on Saturday, November 19, 1960, sixteen months after I showed him the article. Dad was the local veterinarian, and he took a call to attend to an injured cow on a nearby farm. My older brother, Richard, and I both loved riding with Dad on medical calls. The farms, the animals, the medicine were always interesting, but there was also the possibility we would stop along the way to hunt or fish. It was bow hunting deer season, and all three of us kept our bows and arrows stashed in his car. Dusk was approaching, and I knew there was a possibility we could spot a deer in a field and have a chance for a shot. Richard wasn't home yet, but I was in the room when Dad took the call. I asked if I could go along.

"Cow cut her udder on a broken fence," Dad said. "Couple of stitches and I'm done. Nothing you haven't seen before. Why don't you do your Sunday school lesson now? Then we'll have time after dinner to make hunting plans for tomorrow." I couldn't really argue the point, so I agreed.

It was just past 5:00 p.m., and I was sitting at the dining room table finishing my Sunday school lesson, the Holy Bible open on the table before me. My mother was in the kitchen fixing dinner. Richard was in the living room entertaining himself and our baby brother Michael with a game of coochy-coochy-coo. Four-year-old Roger immersed himself in his own fantasy world within the kneehole of Dad's desk. The doorbell rang.

"I'll get it," I called out and skipped over to the front door. When I opened the door, there was the minister of our church, a close family friend, with tears streaming down his face. I was immediately frightened by this image, and I ran, before either of us spoke a word, to the back of the house to find my mother.

"Mom!" I cried with fear in my voice and tears running down my cheeks. "Reverend Hanson is at the door and he's crying." I didn't even know why I was crying yet. I just knew something unspeakable must have happened.

My mother grabbed a kitchen towel to dry her hands as she quickly walked to the front of the house. I stayed on her heels. Rev. Hanson stood in the center of our living room sobbing. My mother began to cry and shake uncontrollably. The minister gathered her up in his arms and brought her to the big stuffed chair. I knelt beside her and the three of us just continued to cry. My mother kept saying, "No, no, no," but no one else said a word. Richard continued to take care of the baby because he knew he couldn't abandon him to experience his own grief. I don't know how he did it. Little Roger came over and asked why we were crying. Mom asked Richard to bring Michael over and she tried to put her arms around all four of her boys. There has been a terrible accident, she told us. Richard and I just said, I know, I know. My mother and Reverend Hanson both cradled us in their arms.

This moment remains frozen in time for me. I do not know how long it lasted. It lasted forever. The loss of my father's voice became a raging silence. The weight of his guiding hand on my shoulder vanished.

Then the neighbors and family friends started to come over. Already they were bringing food for us. Women must have brought the meals they just prepared for their own families because there wasn't time for them to have heard the news and then cooked more food. The house was full of people. I was a wreck. My world had just shattered.

A neighbor woman who knew our family well took me aside, leaned in close to my face, and whispered, "Don't cry in front of your mother anymore. This is going to be very difficult for her, and you need to show her how strong you are." I hated that woman. I knew how difficult this already was for our whole family. I also knew it was okay for me to cry. I wasn't going to waste my breath explaining it to her, though. I just walked away. I cried myself to sleep for a year.

Eventually my mother sent me to bed. Overwhelmed by but also exhausted by my emotions, I slept fitfully, tossing and turning. Lying in bed I realized that my father's fatal crash was my fault. If I simply insisted he let me ride along on his call, I just knew I would have been able to prevent the accident. I could have screamed, "Look out!" or grabbed the steering wheel so we swerved out of the path of danger. Or I could have perished in the crash with him. Anything would have been better than to be stuck in this anguish I knew not how to escape. It was my fault. I should have been there for him. What had I done?

It's not easy for me to recount this event, but it is necessary because it was a major turning point in my life. I remember what it is like for an eleven-year-old boy to be happy. I do not know what it is like for a happy eleven-year-old to grow up. I do know what it is like for an eleven-year-old to grow up with a hole in his heart after his father dies. It's not as if no happiness ever comes my way. I have experienced many happy moments in my life. But the sadness never goes completely away.

This knowledge remained at the forefront of my opposition to the war in Vietnam. Knowing the pain a family endures after the sudden loss of a loved one made it unbearable for me to witness the relentless progression of death brought on by the prosecution of a war increasingly devoid of any value or purpose to the people being killed or the people being left behind. I still come to tears if I dwell on my father's death, just as the loved ones of our soldiers killed in Vietnam must also feel their losses to this day. Those loved ones include sons, daughters, wives, husbands, mothers, fathers, brothers, sisters, grandparents, aunts, uncles, nieces, nephews, cousins, friends, and lovers who must number in the millions. Their losses are unfathomable.

2

JFK's Inaugural Address

January 20, 1961
Ten Dead

In three weeks I would turn twelve. I was still reeling from my father's death, but I was thankful to be back in school where I could experience some sense of normalcy. My classmates and teachers all felt stunned as well; that's how it is in a small town when a man as well known and popular as my father dies suddenly and tragically. But I did feel the compassion and caring from all of them.

One day in January our whole fifth-grade class went to my classmate Darrel's house, less than a block from the school, to watch the new president's inauguration. I don't know how the arrangements were made, but Darrel's mom must have been one special lady to let the whole fifth-grade class into her home. We filled it up sitting on the couch, the chairs, and the floor as we crowded around the family's black and white television set. The boys were practicing their usual bump and shove routine as they jockeyed for the best seats. The girls were trying to act more grown up, but somehow they managed to end up with the best seats. I remember sitting on the floor.

Vietnam was not on our minds. I don't even remember thinking about it much since the first time I read about the two soldiers being killed. Now we were just excited about the new, handsome young president. Our image of a president was one of an old man: Eisenhower, Truman, Roosevelt. They looked like grandfathers to us. This president was about the same age as many of our fathers. We had participated in mock campaigns and elections leading up to this moment, and for the first time in our lives we had been paying genuine attention to politics. I was particularly interested in Robert Frost's appearance at the inauguration because I was starting to take an interest in poetry (although this was not something a fifth-grade boy discussed with his football buddies). I liked the intensity of idea and emotion conveyed by some of the poems we studied in preparation for the day's events. I wondered what this old master would come up with in celebration of this bright young rising star.

First, of course, came the invocation, blessing, and prayer by various religious leaders and a stunning rendition of the national anthem by Marian Anderson. We could already see how cold and windy it was and how brightly the sun was shining and reflecting off the new fallen snow. When Frost took the stage, it was really no surprise he immediately had trouble reading his new poem. His papers fluttered in the wind as he shuffled and angled them trying to see the words. The new vice president, Lyndon Johnson, stepped up and tried to cover the glare with his top hat, but Frost took the hat away and said, "I'll handle that." He made an apology for not being able to see the new poem and immediately began to recite one of his previously published poems, "The Gift Outright," from memory. I was impressed. The old poet was masterful as he turned his inauspicious beginning into a stirring moment.

Then Kennedy took the oath of office. As he stepped to the podium, his charisma compelled the attention of our whole class. I liked this president. I voted for him in our mock elections. I wanted and expected only good things to come from his time in office.

I listened thoughtfully as he delivered a speech that has gone down in history as one of the finest presidential inaugural addresses. But I was not happy with everything he had to say. When he said, "Let every nation know, whether it wishes us well or ill, that we shall pay any price, bear any burden, meet any hardship, support any friend, oppose any foe to assure the survival and success of liberty," I thought he seemed to be doing a bit of chest thumping, stirring up animosities somewhere. I was barely beginning to grasp the complexity of world politics at this point, but I had the feeling he was laying down the gauntlet. Near the end of his talk, when he expressed what are undoubtedly the most famous lines of this speech, "And so, my fellow Americans: ask not what your country can do for you—ask what you can do for your country," I felt troubled again. I could not argue with his call to service. I believed in service to one's country and one's community and one's school and one's neighbors and one's friends and one's family absolutely. But I did not understand why he presented citizens' service as an antithesis to government accountability. (I'm sure at eleven years old I did not know that his use of "antithesis" was a rhetorical device, but I could grasp that he was contrasting the two ideas.) My concept of government was very strongly rooted in the idea government was "of the people, by the people, and for the people." Consequently, the people have every right to ask the government to serve their interests, and if government should fail them or falter in its commitment to the people, the people have every right to remove government officials from office. If they serve the people, the people will gladly serve the government. Perhaps I was naïve. I mention these ideas here simply to lay the groundwork for the thinking that would lead me to action later.

3

WHITE HOUSE PRESS CONFERENCE

January 15, 1962
27 Dead

From the transcript of the press conference available at the John F. Kennedy Presidential Library:

REPORTER: Mr. President, are American troops now in combat in Viet Nam?

PRESIDENT KENNEDY: No.

This is the only mention of Vietnam in the entire press conference. It seems perfectly reasonable to me to expect that some reporter might have had the inquisitiveness to ask the question, "With twenty-seven Americans killed thus far, Mr. President, how many more American lives are you willing to lose in this fight?" But none did.

Which president among the five who presided over the war could have said, "Oh, I don't know, somewhere just over 58,000 American lives, I think that would be my limit"? Certainly one way to hold political leaders accountable is for journalists to ask them tough questions. (My own answer to this question has always been, "Two is too many.")

Here are the numbers of American deaths in Vietnam during each president's term in office:

Eisenhower:	10
Kennedy:	164
Johnson:	37,389
Nixon:	20,587
Ford:	63
TOTAL:	58,213

Astute readers may notice this total falls 73 names short of the 58,286 names on the Vietnam Veterans Memorial Wall. These additional deaths occurred after the end of the war but were directly attributed to injuries incurred during deployment in Vietnam.

4

Cuban Missile Crisis

October 16, 1962
72 Dead

Troop strength in Vietnam gradually increased from 700 soldiers in 1959 to 11,000 by the close of 1962. They were then still serving only in an advisory role. The Vietnam insurgency was not in the headlines every day, and when it did make the news, reporters referred to it as a conflict, not a war.

What was making headlines was The Cuban Missile Crisis. At thirteen years of age I was transfixed by the images on the news depicting the confrontation between Kennedy and Khrushchev as they squared off in a battle of wills that could have ended in the annihilation of all of us. It is bizarre remembering these images. Because television was still in its infancy, or maybe its toddler stage, there was no video footage from the front lines of this clash as there would be today, no satellite photos of the battleships at sea; newsmen literally stood in front of a flat map of the world and moved by hand little construction paper cutouts of Russian ships as they inched across the Atlantic toward paper cutouts of the ships in the U.S. naval blockade around Cuba.

As silly as those images may seem today, they were frightening to us then because we all understood a mistake by either side could result in all-out nuclear war. Those of us who were teenagers in the early Sixties grew up in the Fifties being taught to "duck and cover" in an inane attempt to save ourselves if we ever saw the flash of a nuclear explosion. In school we practiced bomb drills during which we grabbed our winter coats off their classroom hooks and covered our heads with them as we huddled in the hallways waiting for the building to collapse around us. I always wondered how my coat could protect me from the falling bricks, beams, glass, and fire that would follow an atomic blast. Although instructed not to peek out from under our coats during these drills, I always did. I wanted to see the end if it was coming. This is probably when the kids in my generation first began to doubt the adults and think for ourselves. We knew better than to hope for survival. Nuclear war would be the end of everything. There was fear and I think a little resentment, too, toward the two world leaders so callously bringing all of us to the precipice. When the air cleared and the sides completed their secret deals, I moved ever closer to distrusting politicians in general.

5

THE BURNING BUDDHIST

June 11, 1963
120 Dead

Horrifying. The photograph by Malcolm Brown showing the Buddhist monk in the lotus position completely engulfed in flames quickly made its way around the world and shocked everyone who saw it. Although the monk's suicide was a protest, it was not a protest against the Vietnam War or American involvement in it. It was a protest demanding religious freedom and equal treatment for Vietnamese Buddhists who made up 70 to 90 percent of the population: the government of Ngo Dinh Diem had instituted policies beneficial to Catholics regarding public service and military promotions. Catholics also received preference in the distribution of land under land reform laws and the allocation of taxes. Looting and destruction of Buddhist pagodas was common while the government didn't intervene. And how did our government justify our support for a religious minority oppressing a religious majority?

Anti-communism. This was the only reason our political leaders had to justify our presence in Vietnam. The domino theory of communist expansion, first presented by Eisenhower but now supported by Kennedy, seemed an insufficient argument to me. I wondered now about Kennedy's inaugural admonition, "that we shall pay any price, bear any burden, meet any hardship, support any friend, oppose any foe to assure the survival and success of Liberty," How could we call Diem a friend? Whose liberty were we defending here? By the end of the year, four more Buddhist monks perished in the same manner as Thich Quang Duc. There must be, I surmised, very serious problems in Vietnam to compel people to such drastic measures.

Our support of Diem's regime was obviously not about assuring "the survival and success of Liberty," as Kennedy pledged. It was actually about combatting an ideological opponent, nothing more. For me it did not meet the requirements for us to "bear any burden." It seemed odd to me that I, a 14-year-old boy, could parse the difference, but our leaders could not. I knew there must to be forces at play beneath the surface. I just didn't know. what they were.

6

MLK's "Dream" Speech

August 28, 1963
138 Dead

Growing up in Caledonia, Minnesota in the 1960s did not provide me with any first-hand experience in cultural diversity. In all of Houston County there were only two black people, a couple of men who worked at the barrel stave mill halfway between Caledonia and Eitzen, nestled in the hills of the Driftless Area (untouched by glaciers) and surrounded by hardwood forest. I might pass them on the street from time-to-time in downtown Caledonia, and they would greet me with a friendly "hello," as anyone in a small town would, and I'd come back with a "How-ya-doing," but we never felt compelled to stop and chat. Such was the extent of my experience with people of color before I moved to the big city for college.

Still, the civil rights movement made a serious impression on me. The images and stories in the newspapers and on television of black people being beaten by club-wielding police, attacked by police dogs, knocked off their feet by water cannons, and dragged off and thrown into police vans all because they wanted to order a sandwich at a lunch counter, ride a bus, or go to school were incomprehensible to me. When I asked the adults in my life why these things were happening, I was all too often told that we, the people living in the North, did not know what it was like living with negroes (the terms "blacks" and "African Americans" were not yet current), hence we were in no position to judge. I didn't buy it. I could see the ugliness of racism. I could also see the humanity in the faces of the young men at the Woolworths' lunch counter in North Carolina as they continued their sit-in day after day. I admired the courage of six-year-old Ruby Bridges escorted by U.S. Marshals as she marched through a heartless mob shouting and throwing things at her on her way to her first day of classes at William Frantz Elementary School in New Orleans. In October of 1962, President Kennedy sent 5,000 federal troops to suppress the riots as James Meredith became the first black student to enroll at the University of Mississippi. During the early 1960s, student sit-ins would become a vital strategy throughout the south in integrating parks, swimming pools, theaters, libraries, and other public facilities. I duly noted how people could effect change through protest.

I found it hard to believe one hundred years after the Civil War that people who were once enslaved still needed to fight for so much. This is what made the civil rights movement very compelling to me. While I observed these events from the safety of my small town in Minnesota, the dangers faced by black protesters and the white supporters who joined them in voter registration drives and freedom rides echoed through the news stories on our TVs and in our newspapers. Protesters, black and white, died in the pursuit of justice. Innocent children attending church died in prayer. Sometimes the known perpetrators would go unpunished for years. In the middle of all the violence and hatred emerged a man of dedication, courage, and eloquence. I began to read what I could find of Dr. Martin Luther King, Jr.'s words. His commitment to peaceful, nonviolent protest in the face of death threats became the very definition of heroic for me. Learning about Dr. King led me to read more about Mahatma Gandhi, which reminded me to reread Thoreau. Now I possessed the beginnings of a foundation in the tactics and strategies of nonviolent protest. At the age of fourteen, though, I was not yet aware of how soon I would become immersed in this rich tradition. By soon, of course, I mean in five years, which to a fourteen-year-old is an eternity away. Vietnam was still barely a blip on the radar screen, and it did not yet occur to me that I might someday be drafted to fight there.

The Civil Rights March on Washington in 1963 was very much on the radar, and all three television networks announced plans to cover the march throughout the day (there were only the three networks, ABC, CBS, and NBC and nothing else to speak of; PBS had not even been conceived yet, let alone the cable networks). I decided to watch. School would not be in session until the following Tuesday, but we did have a morning football practice. Afterward I was free to watch the news coverage and hear the speeches.

Watching was intoxicating. It quickly became evident this was the largest protest march in Washington, D.C.'s history. The speeches were stirring, and I remember to this day some of the snippets of those speeches that awakened me. John Lewis told the crowd, "Patience is a dirty and nasty word. We do not want to be free gradually, we want our freedom and we want it now." I could understand his position. Josephine Baker remarked, "I have walked into the palaces of kings and queens and into the houses of presidents. But I could not walk into a hotel in America and get a cup of coffee." I could not understand how this could happen in the land of the free.

While there are many extraordinary lines from King's "I Have a Dream" speech, I was especially moved by, "Again and again we must rise to the majestic heights of meeting physical force with soul force." I had witnessed the stark visual images of the beatings and killings meted out to the protesters, and the depth of their courage awed me with this call to nonviolence.

And then came the entertainers. This was the first time I heard Odetta. Wow, what a voice. This was the first time I saw Bob Dylan (I had heard him on the radio before), and he made me proud to be from Minnesota. Joan Baez I already liked along with Peter, Paul and Mary; and Mahalia Jackson we had listened to in music class. Josh White was new to me and very cool. As the camera panned the crowd the reporters would point out some of the other famous people attending in support of the cause: Paul Newman, Joanne Woodward, Marlon Brando, Ray Charles, Shirley MacLaine, Nina Simone, James Garner, Charlton Heston, and many more.

All in all, this day had a profound influence on me. I struggled with my concept of America as the very symbol of freedom for the world, yet still unable to fulfill its promise for so many of its own citizens. On this day, though, 250,000 protesters showed me there was hope for this promise and a path to its fulfillment.

My father, Edward R. Holland, with a Northern Pike caught while ice fishing, circa 1949. Photographer unknown.

7

BUCK FEVER

November 1, 1963
170 Dead

My dad was a hunter and a fisherman, and that's how he raised his boys. On vacation one summer up at Big Hanging Horn Lake, when I was all of maybe ten years old, Dad, Richard, and I had caught our limit in crappies (twenty-five for each of us) plus some bluegills, perch, and a couple of walleyes, so we had pretty near a hundred fish by noon. My dad then said, "Time for you boys to learn how to clean fish." Dad being a veterinarian, the sight of blood and guts was nothing new to me, and I had watched him clean fish many times. But taking the knife in my own hands was certainly a new experience. The first thing he taught us was how to scale the fish. With a little practice I started to learn how to keep the dorsal fin from sticking me as I scraped the knife blade against the grain of the scales, but not before my hands were pretty sore. Then he showed us how to cut off the head, slit the belly, and pull out the guts. It seemed like we spent more time cleaning these fish than catching them, but then, as we wrapped most of them for the freezer while Mom started frying up the walleye for dinner, I felt some pride in having contributed to our family's store of food.

You could not tell by looking at me, I was a normal looking kid I'm sure, but I did not have the manual dexterity, the fine motor skills, my father and brother both possessed. They both became veterinary surgeons. I did not. Both of them could tie a fly on the banks of a trout stream to match the insects they spotted on the water. The only fly I could tie was in our basement workshop with the aid of a bench vise and a magnifying glass, and the only chance my grotesque creation had to catch a brook trout was to scare it to death. Although I never did like ice fishing very much, I dutifully did it. Please pass the perch.

Hunting was my better game. By the age of ten I could hit a squirrel in the head, saving the meat from any damage, with a .22 caliber rifle and had skinned and gutted rabbits and squirrels on my own, but I had not shot a deer yet. When I turned ten, Dad bought Richard and me our first bow and arrow sets. I received a forty-pound straight bow, which was almost too hard to string, but I could do it. It was a beautiful experience to be in the woods with my dad and learn to track and stalk and stand so still and silent a buck within sight could not even tell I was there. When gun season came, my brother, seventeen months older than me, had just turned twelve, and he was now legal to hunt with a gun. I felt left out, but I was only ten, and you had to be twelve to qualify for a gun license. The next year I was only eleven, and Richard was preparing for his second gun deer season, the most exciting hunting season of them all.

But then we bought our bow hunting licenses, and as I was carefully reading over the extensive rules and regulations, something caught my eye. "Dad," I said, "it says right here bow hunters of any age may hunt during gun season. I just can't carry a gun." "OK," he said, "if you can hit the moving deer target with an arrow from 150 feet, you can come."

Dad and his buddies had a moving deer target they had built out in the country. They constructed a wall eight feet high and eight feet wide and one foot deep with wooden planks and then filled it with concrete. One man could then stand safely behind the wall and crank a bicycle wheel attached to a pulley system conveying their silhouette of a deer along a wire track and back again while the other men shot at it with their guns. We had practiced here before and even though I was pretty good with a stationary target, I had not yet hit the moving deer target with an arrow. I would have eight weeks to practice, though, and I was very determined. On our very first time out to the target, my dad paced off 150 feet, laid down a stick, and said, "This is your spot." He sent Richard down to the wall to turn the bicycle wheel, and I strung my bow. I nocked an arrow and pulled the bowstring back to my ear. "Go!" I yelled to Richard, and the cardboard deer started to run. Almost immediately I let my arrow fly and watched it make a perfect arc right to the heart. I threw both my hands in the air in triumph as I yelled, "Yes! Yes! Yes!" Dad was almost doubled over laughing, but he managed to call out to Richard, "Keep it running!" And then to me, "He's not down yet. You have to shoot him again." I quickly pulled an arrow from my quiver, nocked it, and hit the deer target in the rump. By the time my second arrow hit, my third arrow was ready to go. The target was making its way back to the wall now, with the deer oddly running backwards because the pulley system did not turn the target around, and my third shot caught the silhouette in the belly. It did not matter the second and third shots were not kill shots. The first one was, and any hit was all I needed. I gladly manned the bicycle wheel for the next hour while my father and my brother tried unsuccessfully to duplicate my feat. I didn't shoot anymore because I chose not to ruin a perfect three-for-three. I was officially a member of the hunting party. You would have been hard pressed to point to a happier eleven-year-old boy on the planet that day.

School was not officially closed for deer season, but you could get an excused absence. School rules were not nearly as strict in the1960s, and most of the boys plus a few of the girls were gone on Friday for the three-day hunt. We packed all of our gear in the car the night before. All we had to do in the morning was get up, get dressed, and get in the car by 4:00 a.m. Dad drove us to the Redwood Café where we joined a dining room packed with fellow hunters devouring their eggs, and pancakes, and bacon, and coffee. I was alive with excitement. Then we drove out to a section of woods we scouted during bow season. We knew there were deer in there. I realized even then how the rest of Dad's hunting party might worry about the ability of such a young boy to keep up, so I accepted without question the assignments they gave me. They put me on a stand, not in a tree as hunters often do today, but just on the ground, and told me I was responsible for any deer coming in my area. My bow license allowed me to take a buck or a doe, so I was to shoot any deer I saw. They left me there all day, but somebody did stop by every couple of hours to check on me.

Every sound I heard must certainly be a mighty buck coming my way, and the forest is teeming with sounds when you are alone. This dictated I remain on high alert. I kept an arrow nocked, and I was ready to shoot at every foraging squirrel or flitting chickadee making a sound. In a few hours, exhaustion set in, my mind began to wander, I may even have dozed off for a bit. Dad was the first to check on me, and then later his partner Bud checked in. I had no sightings to report, and Dad told me they had seen two deer on a ridge, but they were too far away to take a shot.

I was not wearing a watch, and it was a cloudy day, so I had lost all sense of time. It was cold. Nothing had happened all day. Then suddenly a crashing sound came rushing toward me and in a flash the mighty buck I'd been dreaming of was standing not fifty feet away. I was sitting on a downed log, my bow with nocked arrow in my left hand. The buck was looking straight ahead, not at me. I had a clear shot, but I would have to raise the bow to take it, and I knew the buck would bolt at the first hint of movement by me. I pulled back the bowstring as I raised the bow and let the arrow fly. I was so focused on the shoulder of the buck I did not even notice the sapling half way between us until I saw the arrow glance off it and sail just over the back of the buck. He must have felt my arrow's feathers tickle his back, and just as quickly as he had appeared, he was gone. And I had my first case of full-blown buck fever. My knees were shaking, my hands were sweating, my breathing was rapid, my heart was pounding. Oh wow.

My dad was the only one of our hunting party to bag a deer that year. I was very proud of him. Even though I didn't even see another deer, I had my shot at a buck and a story I tell to this day. The next year I was legal for gun season, but it would be two more years before I bagged my own trophy.

By then we were hunting with Dad's veterinary partner, Bud, and he would take us to the southern tip of the Big Woods, or what was initially called Le Grand Bois by the French explorers who first encountered it. A temperate hardwood forest once covering 5000 square miles in a diagonal strip across south-central Minnesota, the Big Woods had been mostly cleared for farming, but there were secondary stands that still afforded excellent hunting opportunities and could still be called "Big" in their own right. You could get lost in our section of Big Woods. I know this from experience.

On this fateful day we decided to make one last drive before breaking for lunch. We selected a small "L" shaped stand of woods narrowing to about fifty feet wide right where it crossed a gravel county road into a much bigger section of woods. Our hunting party dropped two standers at this crossing point, and I volunteered for one of the posts. Ron and I took up our positions at the tree line of the big section and watched the drivers as they took the cars down a quarter of a mile where they would enter the "L." I was watching them as they got out of their cars and uncased their shotguns, and then one of them started shooting, firing off three quick rounds before they even took one step off the road. Ron and I took one look at each other and we both knew something would be coming. Fast. We shouldered our guns and I set my sights right on the corner of my side of the trees. I could hear every breath I was taking. In an instant the biggest, grandest buck I had ever seen leaped into my sights and stopped to check the clearing of the road before crossing. I barely had to move my gun at all to put

Photo by Richard Holland.

my bead on his left front shoulder, and then I gently squeezed the trigger. At the sound of my shot the buck became airborne as he flew across the road in maybe three bounds. I couldn't believe I had missed him. He was no more than fifty feet away from me when I fired, but I managed to get off two more shots before he disappeared into the next woods. I heard at least two shots from Ron as well. How could we not have dropped him?

I immediately ran to the spot where he had stood when I first shot him expecting to find a large amount of blood. Nothing. "There is no way I missed him," I yelled to Ron. "He was standing still, and my sights were right on him. How could he not fall right here?"

Ron had run to the middle of the gravel road and was looking for signs of blood. He was as excited as I was and said, "I know! No way we both missed him." I joined his search for some sign on the road, but there was nothing. As Ron left the road searching the edge of the woods where the buck must have entered, I ran back to the spot where the buck was when I first spotted him. While carefully examining the forest floor, I moved cautiously so as not to disturb any evidence, and then I saw it: a single leaf with two tiny drops of fresh, bright red blood.

"Got it!" I yelled, picked up the leaf and ran across the road to show Ron.

"Now we know he's hit," he said. "We'll find him."

Just then we heard another shot from the drivers, so we got back in our crouches in case another deer attempted to cross to the bigger woods. In a few minutes the rest of our party emerged from the trees. Their first question was "Where's the big buck?"

"He's hit," I said. "We've got a trail right over here."

We set up a line six across and entered the woods, each of us looking for signs. There would be a few drops of blood, then a spurt, and finally a large spray. You could see he was seriously wounded. We trailed him a good two hundred yards into some dense brush where we found him dead. He was the most magnificent eight-point buck I have ever seen, before or since, and would dress out at 195 pounds. As we examined the carcass, we found a single bullet wound just behind the left shoulder, right where I had placed the bead of my shotgun as I squeezed the trigger. Ron agreed it was my kill.

"I hope your knife is sharp," Bud said.

"It is. It is," I said, and I took off my outer shell of hunters orange, and then my coat, and then my vest, and then my long sleeve thermal undershirt till I was down to just a t-shirt. This was going to be messy. Bud Karli, my dad's veterinary partner, whom I had known all my life, was the best teacher a kid could want to talk him through his first field dressing of a deer. After I slit the belly all the way up to the sternum, I reached up inside the neck as far as I could and cut off the esophagus and windpipe. As I started to pull the entrails out, I found what was left of the heart. The 12-gauge shotgun slug I shot him with had blown the top of the heart completely away. We were all amazed this buck had been able to run two hundred yards from the road without a beating heart.

My thanks to Richard for helping me drag him out to the road. It was a cool autumn day, but I stayed in my t-shirt and still worked up a sweat with the effort. As we were tying the buck onto Bud's vehicle, another small hunting party drove by and stopped to admire our trophy. One of the men asked who shot him. As the only member of our hunting party standing on the road in a t-shirt with arms still bloodied to the elbows, I said, "Who do you think shot him?" At fourteen I had killed my first buck. Now I was a man.

By the age of sixteen I had killed three whitetail deer. But the guilt I felt with each kill finally overtook the pride I experienced, and I had to stop the killing. I didn't want to become a vegetarian, or even give up eating venison. It was just the sight of a big whitetail buck in his full glory in the forest was such a beautiful vision it seemed wrong for me to end the animal's life by squeezing the trigger of my 12-gauge shotgun and sending a lead slug crashing through the buck's flesh, shattering bones and destroying vital organs. So I gave up hunting with a gun. For the next few years I hunted only with bow and arrows and took my pleasure from the game of wits with my quarry. One farmer who knew my father well told me about a big buck she had seen on her farm several times, and I spent the next two years tracking him, learning his habits, trying to anticipate his next move. When I was finally close enough for a shot, I simply exposed myself to the animal and watched him bound away. He was a sight to behold. Then I gave up hunting altogether.

8

Ngo Dinh Diem Assassinated

November 2, 1963
170 Dead

This news about Diem's assassination made headlines, maybe not the at top of the page, but still on the front page. I was so young and innocent, the news shocked me. I read through the newspaper articles to see if they could help me make sense of it. There were just hints at some of the problems that would be well documented years later, but there was enough troubling information about our government's involvement to make me question why we would remain in Vietnam at all.

I had learned of Diem's repressive policies against the majority Buddhists the previous June when the Buddhist monks began setting themselves on fire, but that hadn't prepared me for Diem's assassination. The Buddhists, of course, had nothing to do with the actual assassination, but their continued protests had been instrumental in destabilizing Diem's regime. Members of his own military deposed him in a coup, and the next day shot and killed him and his brother, Ngo Dinh Nhu, in the back of a truck. Now it was being revealed the United States had lost all faith in Diem's ability to maintain control in South Vietnam. The newspaper quoted unnamed sources saying the U.S. government felt relieved by the coup. There were also hints they actually sanctioned the assassination. Congressman Clement J. Zablocki from neighboring Wisconsin said he was convinced "there must have been some encouragement" by United States authorities. Several military coups would follow one after the other during the next few years. There would never be a government established in South Vietnam we would be able to point to with pride and say, "We are defending their liberty," and be believable.

It's quite sad that our elected leaders could not see or would not admit to the folly they engaged in. It was clear to me, a fourteen-year-old boy, that this fight was not about the reasons our government publicly proclaimed. If only someone in authority would have said, "ENOUGH" at this point, a great national tragedy could have been averted. Instead, another 58,116 Americans would lose their lives.

9

JFK Assassinated

November 22, 1963
174 Dead

Havoc. Catastrophe. Devastation. No single word could encompass the utter chaos, the emotional turmoil, following the assassination of John Kennedy. I had been troubled by the use of assassination as a political tool in tiny, distant South Vietnam, but I had never imagined, in my youthful naiveté, that assassination was a possibility here in the United States of America.

Even though I had begun to differ with some of the philosophical statements the young president had made, I liked him. He oozed charisma. To my knowledge, all of the presidents before him had been old men. Here was a young man ready to lead a vibrant nation into the modern world. And of course, my heart went out to his young children and his wife, whose pain must have rendered their hearts asunder.

I was in my eighth-grade geography class when the news swept through the school. An announcement came over the intercom: President Kennedy had just been shot and school was now closed for the day. We were in shock. It took me fifteen minutes to walk home where my mother was already sitting in front of the television. The news coverage went wall to wall for the first time in my life, and I could not look away. I watched Walter Cronkite, probably the most trusted man in America, a father figure to the nation, with tears in his eyes as he reported, "From Dallas, Texas, the flash apparently official, President Kennedy died at 1:00 p.m. Central

Standard Time, two o'clock Eastern Standard Time, some 38 minutes ago. [There was an emotional pause lasting six very long seconds.] Vice President Johnson has left the hospital in, ah, Dallas, but we do not know, ah, to where he has proceeded. Presumably, he will be taking the oath of office shortly and become the 36th President of the United States."

Regular programming would not resume until Tuesday, November 26th, the day after the President's funeral.

Glued to the television, I watched in horror as Jack Ruby shot and killed Lee Harvey Oswald during a live broadcast on Sunday morning. The rest of my family had gone to church, but I could not stop watching the news. What the hell was happening to the world? The conspiracy theories began immediately and have not subsided to this day.

None of this really made me think of Vietnam at the time, but it certainly started me down the path of mistrust and doubt when it came to government. While I do not subscribe to any particular conspiracy theory, I still do not believe the American people know with any certainty all of the information concerning this national tragedy. We may never know the truth.

Back in 1963, I struggled to grasp the enormity of our nation's loss. I felt sadness, fear, confusion. Anxiety overwhelmed me. I seriously asked myself, "What kind of world am I living in?"

10

Gulf of Tonkin Resolution

August 7, 1964
309 Dead

Football was my main concern that day. I would begin my freshman year in high school in a few weeks, but two-a-day practices had already started for the football team. I knew I would make the team and suit-up for games, but my goal was to become one of the few players to win a school letter as a freshman. In pursuit of my goal, I had checked out half-a-dozen books on football from the La Crosse public library at the beginning of the summer (La Crosse was the nearest city to Caledonia and had a more extensive library). I was already fairly knowledgeable about football with four years of organized participation behind me. Now my intent was to be the smartest player on the field, and maybe not the biggest or the strongest, but certainly the toughest.

I began with isometric exercises the moment my eyes opened in the morning, followed by precise stretches and calisthenics designed to max-imize every movement I made as I rose from bed, dressed, and moved through the morning rituals. One hour of running preceded breakfast, and then a run across town to my summer job working at the public swimming pool. My friend Bill and I were in charge of cleaning the locker rooms, run-ning the pool filters, and mowing the grass for the regulation baseball field, little league field, and picnic areas. We did not have riding mowers. We had walk-behind gas powered mowers, thus a day of work was always a day of exercise. There was so much grass to mow that by the time we finished cutting it, we had to start cutting again. At the end of the day, we would go for a swim. Then I would run home. In the evening, after the pool had closed, I would sneak my girlfriend in for a moonlight swim. All of this was for football. I wanted to keep the body moving, push it to its limit. At the end of a football game when all the players on the field were running out of gas, I would be the one with something left in the tank. My plan worked. When the season opened, I started at middle linebacker, assuring my varsity letter.

Caught up as I was in my idyllic teenage life of football and moonlight swims, you might think I wouldn't even notice something like the Gulf of Tonkin Resolution. But it was headline news and I was still an avid newspaper reader. While I did not think about Vietnam every single day (there would come a time, soon, when we all did), I had not forgotten reading about the two soldiers killed when I was ten. Now at the age of fifteen my mind couldn't comprehend this. The Gulf of Tonkin Resolution granted unprecedented power to a president to engage in military action in foreign countries without a declaration of war. I was appalled that only two senators had the courage and the wisdom to vote against the resolution. Senators Ernest Gruening and Wayne Morse were heavily criticized, but their reasoning made so much sense to me I could not understand the sheer ignorance of the rest of the politicians. Their words are worth remembering here. (SOURCE: Congressional Record. August 6-7, 1964. Pp18132-33, 18406-7, 18458-59, and 18470-71.):

"MR. GRUENING: [Ernest Gruening, D–Alaska] . . . Regrettably, I find myself in disagreement with the President's policy. . . The serious events of the past few days, the attack by North Vietnamese vessels on American warships and our reprisal, strikes me as the inevitable and foreseeable concomitant and consequence of U.S. unilateral military aggressive policy in Southeast Asia. . . . We now are about to authorize the President if he sees fit to move our Armed Forces . . . Not only into South Vietnam, but also into North Vietnam, Laos, Cambodia, Thailand, and of course the authorization includes all the rest of the SEATO nations. That means sending our American boys into combat in a war in which we have no business, which is not our war, into which we have been misguidedly drawn, which is steadily being escalated. This resolution is a further authorization for escalation unlimited. I am opposed to sacrificing a single American boy in this venture. We have lost far too many already . . .

"MR. MORSE: [Wayne Morse, Dem.-Ore.] . . . I believe that history will record that we have made a great mistake in subverting and circumventing the Constitution of the United States . . . I believe this resolution to be a historic mistake. I believe that within the next century, future generations will look with dismay and great disappointment upon a congress which is now about to make such a historic mistake."

Thank you, gentlemen. Let the record also indicate the "facts" about the "attacks" on the American ships, used by President Johnson to justify this resolution, would eventually be discredited by independent investigations conducted by the military and Congress. How easy it was, and remains to this day, for politicians to lie. The Gulf of Tonkin Resolution itself came to an end when Congress repealed it on January 12, 1971. Another 3,404 American soldiers would die in Vietnam after that date.

The War Powers Resolution became effective on November 7, 1973, after both houses of Congress voted to override President Nixon's veto of the long overdue law still limiting today (but not eliminating) the president's power to engage the military in hostilities without the approval of Congress.

11

FIRST COMBAT TROOPS DEPLOYED

February 9, 1965
450 Dead

My focus on the morning of February 9th was one hundred percent on passing my first road test. I was a confident driver. Two summers earlier I was hanging out with Bill and Art, my friends and co-workers, both a couple years older than me, and one day Bill said to Art, "Hey! Let's teach Danny to drive!" I certainly had no objection. They baptized me in Art's '54 Ford with a three-on-the-tree stick shift. Out on a deserted country road between two fields of tall corn, I sat behind the wheel with the engine off while Art went through the clutching and shifting motions with me. Then it was time to fire up the motor. For the first time, I truly felt the power of a car. The steering wheel vibrated in my grip. I felt like I was about to drive a tank. Then I tried to slowly release the clutch, but the car started lurching forward on me. It was like a bucking bronco, and Art and Bill couldn't stop laughing at me. I managed to get the clutch out and smooth out the acceleration and there I was, driving a car. "Shift to second, shift to second," Art was saying, and I managed to do so with a minimum of grinding. There was no shoulder to the road at all, just a steep incline down ten feet to the bottom of the ditch. I was definitely concerned about the ditch. "Shift to third," Art instructed me, and I managed a smooth transition. With the increased speed, minimal as it was, I felt like I was flying. There was a lot of play in the steering wheel as it rocked back and forth, and I was unsure how I was keeping the car straight. I was keeping my eye on the ditch, too. A curve in the road was coming up and I expressed some trepidation. "Slow down a little with the brake, listen to the engine, now shift down to second," Art coached me, having me double clutch because the old beater had no synchronizers in her tranny, and I kept the car under control around the curve. This was exhilarating. Art and Bill let me drive wherever we went the rest of the summer. We all worked together at the swimming pool, which meant I was driving almost every day. I got pretty good at it. The next summer I took the required driver's ed course, but the teacher always cut my hour short because, he said, "You already know how to drive."

But now I had to take the road test. A test could always make me nervous no matter how prepared I thought I was, especially a skill test. Now add in the competitive nature of small-town teens. Passing the test was not enough. If you didn't score above 90, you would be teased as a lousy driver. But I had confidence. I had been driving for a year and a half now, and my mom's car was much easier to handle than Art's. I backed out of the garage, my mother riding shotgun, pulled up to the first corner, and signaled for a left turn. Nothing happened. I tried the right signal. Nothing again. I tried the emergency flashers. Still nothing. There was no other car available and no time to stop somewhere hoping for a quick fix. My appointment was in ten minutes, so we just drove there and checked-in. When the examiner called my name, I explained my turn signals had quit working on the way to the test and asked if he could reschedule me for later in the day while I went to get the signals fixed. He said, "No. You'll just have to take the test using hand signals."

It was a balmy 23 degrees, not bad for February in Minnesota. Still, it sucked. In spite of the nerves, the competition, the freezing left hand, I managed to score a 92. Not the best of any of my classmates, but good enough to win praise instead of ridicule. The main thing for me was I had my driver's license. Real independence was now within my grasp. I could actually be alone with a girl. The potential was intoxicating.

So, there was a great deal on my mind that day. Vietnam was always in the back of my mind, simply because my heart ached for the soldiers who were dying and the families who were losing them. But I had just turned sixteen, and I had a girlfriend and a set of car keys. Forgive me if I was distracted.

From my vantage point now, I can glance back and note that *The New York Times* published an unsigned editorial the day I passed my test titled, "The Dangers in Vietnam . . ." The editorial pointed out "President Johnson has in the past denied that the United States has any intention of carrying the war to North Vietnam." (The President's intentions would change in one month when he launched a massive bombing campaign against North Vietnam.) The Times went on to state, "The only sane way out is diplomatic, international, political, economic—not military . . . and 'victory' by either side is impossible." This was a bold statement at a time when polls showed 80% of Americans supported the war, due in large part to their Cold War fear of world domination by the communists. With 450 U.S. casualties in Vietnam already, we had a major newspaper calling for a diplomatic end to the crisis. Instead, Johnson authorized deployment of a U.S. Marine Corps Hawk air defense missile battalion, the first commitment of American combat troops in South Vietnam. The 3,500 troops would arrive in Da Nang on March 8, and by the end of the year we would have 200,000 soldiers fighting in South Vietnam.

12

OPERATION ROLLING THUNDER

March 2, 1965
489 Dead

President Johnson authorized his bombing campaign of North Vietnam and ordered over 100 fighter-bombers to attack targets on the first day. This I took notice of. We had newspaper headlines and television footage showing us what seemed like a massive attack. We could watch the bombs falling from our planes and exploding on their targets while we sat on our couches in our comfy living rooms. This was the first time an American war was brought home this vividly, quickly, and graphically. While the news coverage was not often slanted toward an antiwar position, especially in the early days, the images themselves began to fuel growing public opposition. It would take a few more years before opposition to the war broke the 50% level in national polls, but watching the bombs explode was gut wrenching from the beginning.

What President Johnson initially intended to be an eight-week assault to weaken the resolve of the North Vietnamese became instead the longest sustained aerial bombing campaign in American history, at the time, lasting more than three-and-a-half years; and it did not deter the North Vietnamese. As an indication of how obsessed the Johnson Administration was with Vietnam, the politicians and their civilian staff attempted to micromanage this air war even down to the selection of targets for the thousands of sorties flown.

At sixteen years old, I just wanted to live the life teenagers are meant to live: dating, sports, studies, hunting, fishing, more dating. If I didn't have a date, I would jump in a car with some buddies, and we would drive around town looking for girls to talk to. Gas was so cheap in those days that five guys could each chip-in a dime and buy enough gas to cruise around all night. It was a carefree existence.

But then the bombs exploded on the television screen when the late night news came on, while I was safe at home and curled up with my trusted Springer Spaniel, The Duchess. I would watch in horror as entire buildings would disappear in a ball of fire and smoke. I knew there had to be people in those buildings whose lives were ended and whose families' lives were forever disrupted, and I was not so carefree anymore.

13

Torched

August 3, 1965
489 Dead

Millions of Americans experienced a combination of shock, dismay, and outrage when they witnessed U.S. Marines setting fire to peasant homes in the hamlets of Cam Ne south of Da Nang, as reported by Morley Safer on the CBS Evening News. I was among them. I watched as our soldiers pushed and pulled old men, women, and children from their thatched roof huts and then set those huts ablaze with cigarette lighters and flamethrowers. Agonized expressions of fear and dismay marked the faces of the peasants as they begged and pleaded with the soldiers to stop. Morley Safer reported, "Every, every house that I could see, as far as I could see," was burned to the ground.

When the operation concluded, the day's tally stood at 150 homes destroyed, three Vietnamese women wounded, one Vietnamese baby killed, one U.S. marine wounded, and four old Vietnamese men taken prisoner. Americans had never before witnessed their own soldiers acting in such a brutal manner. Now we were watching this atrocity on the TV screens in our own living rooms. We were more accustomed to watching World War II movies where the American soldiers rode in on their jeeps and tanks, saved the village from the bad guys, and then handed out chocolates to the children, silk stockings to the women, and cigarettes to the old men.

I felt powerless to stop the soldiers, but I wanted to stop them. I wanted to stand between the soldiers and the thatched roof huts these Vietnamese people had built with their own hands and beg the soldiers not to burn them to the ground. But how could I? I was just sixteen years old and 10,000 miles away. This was very wrong. How could we condone this? How could we do this? Yes, I felt as if our soldiers were doing this in our names at the behest of our government. It would be a couple of years yet before I could forge the courage to take a meaningful stand against this war, but this event created a wrenching emotional chasm in my heart. No amount of government double-speak would ever be able to justify what we just witnessed.

14

Rubber Soul **Released**

December 3, 1965
2,039 Dead

When the Beatles first appeared on The Ed Sullivan Show on February 9, 1964, with all the attendant hoopla, it mystified me why the older generation concerned themselves so much about the boys' hair. If you look today at a picture of the Beatles in 1964, you would say they have short hair. Back then, all of the boys in my high school parted their hair on one side or the other, combed the hair all the way across the top of the head, and then combed the front up in a flip. Hair oil made the hair obey the comb. All the Beatles did was wash their hair out and let it fall naturally down over their foreheads. People called it a mop top. Big deal.

My friend David came to school Monday morning after The Ed Sullivan Show with his hair combed down instead of flipped up, but it really wasn't measurably longer than it had been on Friday afternoon. Such a complicated concept did not enter the thinking of our principal. He told David to comb his hair up or go home. Without hesitating, David went home. I suppose his mother gave him no alternative as he returned to school the same afternoon with his hair in its proper place. The whole thing was laughable to us. A lot of the guys, myself included, started to grow our hair long and use generous amounts of hair oil to keep the hair from falling over our ears, which was also forbidden. Then on the weekends we would wash out the hair oil, flop our heads around, and let our hair fall free. It was great fun. And what did the principal teach us when he suspended David? He taught us not to respect foolish rules or the foolish people who try to enforce them. This was the lesson we took with us throughout the tumult of the decade.

The Beatles went on to change the course of popular music and culture. One of the turning points was the release of *Rubber Soul* in late 1965. I remember staring at the picture on the front of the album cover before I even slipped the record out to put it on the turntable. The words and faces stretched across the cover as if they were made of rubber, and the intimation was the music inside would stretch your soul, your very core, into shapes previously unknown. All this came to me without the benefit of marijuana. I was not aware of any marijuana available in tiny Caledonia at the time. But rumors abounded about the Beatles experimenting with pot during the recording of the album. I really didn't know what influence that could have. I had no idea how smoking marijuana might have affected their music. Then I put the record on.

Lyrically, Rubber Soul represented a major evolution in the Beatles sensibilities as they moved from the silly pop love songs to more sophisticated and thoughtful lyrics and a more grown-up attitude toward relationships. This progression would continue through *Revolver, Sgt. Pepper's Lonely Hearts Club Band*, and the White Album. The instrumentation and resulting sounds also surprised and widened not only the perspectives of their young fans, but of their contemporaries in music as well. Were I to list just the titles of the songs from the Sixties with heavy influence on our lives, it would run to several pages, as there were so many good bands and great songs. If you are younger than me, then the music of your youth will undoubtedly comprise the soundtrack of your life, but the artists of the Sixties will surely have influenced it.

The Beatles would continue to provide relevant music for the soundtrack of our lives throughout the rest of the decade. Here comes "Nowhere Man" (released on the British version of Rubber Soul, but not on the American version; it was later released as a single in February of 1966 and on an American album, Yesterday and Today, in June of 1966). Rubber Soul indeed. It was mind-bending.

15

HEY! HEY! LBJ!

January 12, 1966
2,450 Dead

"To know war is to know that there is still madness in this world." President Lyndon Johnson said so in his State of the Union speech. Did he think only the enemy had gone mad? I doubt it. He knew the madness went both ways. But did he try to stop the madness? No, he did not. And his failure to stop constituted Johnson's madness.

Watching Johnson's speech when I was just sixteen years old, I was struck by the dichotomy between his grand vision for the Great Society at home and his unrelenting dedication to pursuing the war in Vietnam. With troop strength now surpassing 200,000 and the continued bombing of North Vietnam, the body count had begun to climb exponentially. The fact that we did not support a democracy was already well documented: it was no secret we allowed a series of corrupt dictators to run the South Vietnamese government. It troubled me to listen to Johnson say, "We fight for the principle of self-determination—that the people of South Vietnam should be able to choose their own course, choose it in free elections without violence, without terror, and without fear." This was nothing more than a nice sentiment unsupported by facts. The United States had actually prevented free elections to unite the two Vietnams, because it was clear the communists would win. For Johnson to continue the war under these false pretenses was another form of madness.

There are many books and historical documents available today which illustrate and enumerate the myriad miscalculations made inevitable by the massive arrogance of our politicians and the generals who abetted them, all in service to their reputations and careers, not their nation. This arrogance is madness, too.

While the American casualties of this war were unbearable to contemplate and the driving force in my personal fight to end the madness, the losses for the Vietnamese people were incomprehensible. Official estimates put the number between two million and three million dead. It is difficult to count bodies after carpet bombing and napalming. Does this not look like genocide? Look again at the American casualties, and there are estimates the number of suicide deaths by Vietnam veterans now exceeds the 58,286 who died during the war. The injured, maimed, and permanently disabled from both sides reaches into the millions. This is madness.

Johnson may well have gone down in history as one of the greatest presidents if he had just stopped the war. He could have gone on to accomplish all the goals of his Great Society. He would be remembered today as a peacemaker. Granted, South Vietnam would have fallen to the North, and Vietnam would have been reunited under Communist rule, which is how it turned out anyway, but we could have saved over 50,000 American lives and spared over two million Vietnamese lives. It was madness not to do so. Madness is why protesters circled the White House and chanted, "Hey! Hey! LBJ! How many kids did you kill today?"

16

ALI VS. TERRELL

February 6, 1967
9,490 Dead

Muhammad Ali began to influence me in 1960 when he won the light-heavyweight Olympic boxing gold medal as Cassius Clay. "I am the greatest!" he declared, and I found the super-self-confidence of the brash young fighter inspiring. At the ripe old age of eleven, it would take me a couple of years yet to hone my own self-confidence, but Ali was the role model who showed me the way. I decided to believe in my abilities and myself and to put in the effort to back-up my belief. The effort was the key to the confidence.

Effort and confidence were the keys to my success as a high school athlete. Earning a starting slot on both defense and offense in my freshman year of football, plus winning four letters in track and three letters in basketball, might not have happened without the inspiration of this charismatic super athlete and poet. Yes, I wrote poetry as well, but there were no other role models who excelled in their sport and displayed their literary prowess to boot. Muhammad Ali was The Man.

Now on this day, February 6, 1967, my eighteenth birthday, I was officially required to register with the Selective Service System, and Muhammad Ali, who had just had his request for conscientious objector status rejected on appeal, would fight Ernie Terrell in defense of his World Heavyweight Championship. This confluence of events crystallized my own thoughts on my responsibilities as an American citizen.

I sat on the edge of my seat as I listened to the fight on the radio. (The only television broadcast in those days was on closed-circuit TV shown in movie theaters at a price too steep for me.) The announcer told us how Ali began to badger Terrell before the opening bell with taunts of, "What's my name? What's my name?" because Terrell refused to use Ali's new name, referring to his opponent as Cassius Clay. To me Ali's name change meant no more than Robert Zimmerman becoming Bob Dylan or Archie Leach converting to Cary Grant. Terrell paid a price for his obstinacy, though, as Ali toyed with him, purposely not delivering the knockout blow in order to punish Terrell for a full fifteen rounds.

While Ali had reasons to refuse induction beyond any that might apply directly to me—"No Vietcong ever called me nigger" comes to mind—his statements about Vietnam delved deeper than the racial components alone. He talked about the economics of the war abroad versus the poverty at home and the discrimination inherent in the system's deferment policies, which granted exemptions to the privileged youth who could afford to go to college. He may as well have been pointing a finger at me.

So this was the day I realized I was part of the war machine myself. I had to register for the draft or face prosecution. Because I did not want to go to prison before I finished high school, I went ahead and signed the registration papers, the first step we all took, as young men, which allowed the government to conduct a massive war far from home. I was already accepted at the University of Minnesota. I could feel safe with my student deferment for the next four years, by which time the war would certainly end (it did not), but my personal safety did not protect my conscience from knowing others of my generation would be called to fulfill the military's demand for more bodies.

Thus began the crisis of conscience I would alternately struggle with and suppress from my consciousness, to no avail really. The war was always at the forefront of the news now with the death tolls duly counted and calculated on a daily basis. I am not ashamed it would take another year for me to acquire the courage of my convictions. Each of us matures in the face of our own dilemma. My choices were becoming clearer, and my guts would catch-up with my conscience by the end of my first year at the University.

17

GRADUATION

June 2, 1967
13,545 Dead

"My water just broke," my mother said to me as we stood in the canned fruit aisle of the grocery store where we were picking up last minute supplies for the graduation party my mother and stepfather were hosting for friends and family that evening. "You'll have to take me to the hospital right now." It was just after 1:00 p.m. Eight hours later my sister entered the world while I was graduating, and Lisa and I have enjoyed the bond created by this synchronicity ever since.

I had a great time all through high school. Except for the occasional and inevitable break-up with a girlfriend, it was a carefree and happy experience. I excelled in my studies, finishing third in my class. I earned four school letters in football and track and three in basketball. I participated in one-act plays from eighth grade on. I participated in extemporaneous speaking and storytelling in forensics competitions. I was co-captain of the debate team, junior and senior editor of the school newspaper, vice president of the student council, and treasurer of the Luther League. Hunting, fishing, camping, water skiing in the wake of towboats pushing their barges up and down the Mississippi River, and dating filled my leisure hours. Summer weekends exploring the backwater channels of the Mississippi River, in the homemade kayaks my brother Richard and I constructed in our garage, allowed us to feel like Huck Finn and Tom Sawyer. None of this seemed extraordinary to me at the time as most of my high school friends maintained an equal array of extracurricular activities. Such was the opportunity afforded us by life in a small town.

For the first time in our high school's history, the valedictorian and salutatorian would not automatically be giving speeches at graduation. This year the English faculty required every senior to write a speech as an English class assignment and then present the speech before the entire English faculty, which would select the top four speeches for presentation at graduation. Of course, I wanted to be one of the speakers. It would be an honor to address my classmates on our last night together, and I began outlining my ideas for such a speech as soon as the assignment was announced.

I knew my audience, the English faculty, quite well and already enjoyed their respect for my writing and speaking abilities. I figured at least half the class would have a legitimate shot at one of the four spots, which meant I could not approach the task lightly. As I contemplated what might make my effort singular, I hit upon a brilliant idea (I have these frequently, even if they don't always pan out): I would write my speech in iambic pentameter. This, I reasoned, would impress the faculty with my extra effort. And extra effort it was, crafting the essay line by line to find the vocabulary to match the meter and maintain the meaning I hoped to convey. When I finally finished the writing and typed it up, I immediately began to have second thoughts about what I had written. Looking at it on the page, I knew the judges would understand what I had done, but it suddenly seemed rather pretentious of me. I began to worry my format might actually count against me as it went outside the parameters of the stated assignment. I retyped the speech as a prose piece. I figured I could still deliver the speech at the judging from my first typed copy in line form while the judges followed along in the prose version. This way the cadence of the iambic pentameter could still resonate in the judges hearing, but their printed copies would lack any obvious pretension. It worked.

While I definitely enjoyed my moment in the sun at graduation, I dare say none of us spent much time pondering the speeches. I cannot find a copy of the speech today, nor do I clearly remember the specifics of my message beyond my call for my fellow students to prepare themselves to assume leadership of the country. The exhilaration stemming from graduation, and the intriguing prospects of the futures awaiting us, were more than enough to occupy our thoughts. Add to that the birth of my sister and a home full of out-of-town guests, and my mind was spinning.

John, my best buddy in high school, and I were also co-hosting one of several graduation parties after the formal proceedings. We had chosen to bill our party as the alcohol-free event of the evening. It's not as if I never partook of the occasional beer in high school, but drinking was not a big focus of my teen years. John and I had both expressed to each other some concerns about the amount of drinking everyone knew would take place on graduation night. It was a small-town tradition. Together we decided to co-host an alcohol-free party to provide a safe haven for those fellow students not comfortable attending a drinking party. Just about everyone in our class came by our party to share a few laughs before going on to other festivities, and a solid core stayed well into the night before finally fading away. I wonder if one particular girl remembers a kiss good night. I still do.

18

First Corporate Lie

July 4, 1967
14, 624 Dead

Before 7:00 a.m. the morning after I graduated, I boarded a train to the Twin Cities. Not because there was any trouble at home or I didn't love my hometown, but simply because the excitement of life in the big city beckoned. I was crashing on the floor of my brother Richard's dorm room while he finished up his finals week, and then we would look for an apartment to share for the summer. I began searching the newspaper want ads for potential summer jobs.

"Conduct educational interviews. No experience necessary," the ad read. There was no phone number, just an address on Lake Street in Minneapolis. This sounded like something I could do. I was interested in education, and I had no experience. Certainly I knew how to talk to people, though. This could be my big break. Hey, I decided, living in the big city is going to be easier than I thought.

Richard's dorm room was on the University of Minnesota St. Paul campus, so I had to get up before daylight in order to make the bus connections that would get me to the Lake Street address early enough to be among the first interviewed for the job. After filling out the application, I waited with a handful of other applicants for my turn to interview. A tall, well-dressed man in his mid-thirties with slightly long blond hair swept back over his head and a vice grip for a handshake called me into his office. I had listed my array of high school accomplishments, and my interviewer seemed pleased. We quickly established a friendly rapport, and I started to feel confident he would hire me. He concluded the interview by saying they would continue to meet with people today and Tuesday and I could expect a call back on Wednesday with a yes or a no. Would I be able to start my training on Thursday if I made the grade? Yes, I would.

Thursday morning found me back in the same office, a new hire, and just as pleased as I could be that it had been so easy to find a job. There were an even dozen of us in the office to begin our training, all of us college students, but I was the only freshman-to-be, and therefore the youngest of the bunch. Our leader was the same man who had interviewed me, let's call him Kurt, and he proceeded to explain how we would be working for a company called Colliers Encyclopedia, one of only three major encyclopedias published in English. We would be working directly under the supervision of the advertising department.

One of the new hires raised his hand and asked Kurt, "Why did the ad I answered say we would be 'conducting educational interviews' if we are working for the advertising department?"

"You've asked a good question," Kurt said, and he went on to explain how the company's advertising program worked. We would be going door-to-door in residential neighborhoods looking for a few "qualified families" to place a free set of encyclopedias with. They would use the encyclopedias for one year and then write a letter about how useful they were for their family. This letter would serve as an advertising brochure for the encyclopedia right in their own neighborhood to their neighbors.

"So you see," Kurt said, "in a sense you are conducting educational interviews because we want to place the encyclopedias with families who have an interest in education and will make good use of the books. We want them to write letters of praise, after all."

I can't believe we all bought such crap. We nodded our heads in agreement and accepted the corporate lie. Our training over the next ten days consisted of memorizing and practicing the pitches we would need, from door openers to closings, in order to "place" the "free" encyclopedias in the best homes. I call them "free" encyclopedias because we soon learned the chosen families must show their sincerity in the deal by buying the yearbooks and research service for ten years at a cost of just 35 cents per day. This would amount to the normal retail cost of a set of encyclopedias, but the customers were not informed of this. By the end of my week and a half of training I came to the realization we actually were selling the encyclopedias door-to-door while lying to our customers about the nature of the transaction in order to trick them into the deal. This started to feel creepy to me. The "help wanted" ad lied to me about the true nature of the job. The training seminar lied to me about our motives. Now I was in the field lying to my potential customers.

As it turned out, this was the only method all three of the encyclopedia publishers used to sell their products. In just a few short years the Federal Trade Commission would outlaw the practice, but for now I headed down that dark road full speed ahead. Each day I didn't get up and walk out made it much more difficult to escape the commitment of time and energy already invested.

It all came to a climax when we decided to take a road trip west in order to get away from the metropolitan area where most people had been so inundated with door-to-door sales pitches they had acquired superior sales resistance tactics of their own. My field supervisor suggested we drive to his hometown in Montana and stop at the small towns and country homes along the way where the people would have little or no exposure to traveling salesmen and be easy pickings for us. This was another lie, of course, as the Fuller Brush Co. had a sales force in excess of 17,000 reps blanketing the country. It would be next to impossible to find a door no sales rep had ever knocked on before.

In Wynot, Nebraska, I finally hooked a young mother who lived in a trailer home on the desolate edge of this tiniest of towns. Sure, she just wanted to give her two young toddlers a better education than she had received, so it was easy for her to fall for my line of crap about free encyclopedias. I was just eighteen, and she looked all of nineteen to me with two kids to support and no sign of a man or anyone else in the house to help out, and now she was scurrying around her trailer frantically searching for her checkbook.

"Oh, my God! Oh, my God!" she exclaimed out loud. "The first time in my life I get something for free, and I can't find my checkbook!"

You can imagine the guilt I felt listening to her, but I joined her in the search. I would not get my commission unless I turned in her deposit, so together we tore the inside of the trailer to pieces in search of her checkbook. Once we found it and the check was in my hand, I wished her well and got out of there as quickly as I could, fearing I might succumb to my guilt and return the money to its rightful owner.

Many of the small towns we traveled through on this trek had what were called "Green River ordinances," i.e., laws prohibiting door-to-door solicitations without a permit. My first encounter with such an ordinance came the next night when we stopped in Valentine, Nebraska. My supervisor dropped me off in a quiet residential neighborhood where I would be on my own until my 9:00 p.m. pick-up at our designated location. I began my door-to-door rituals but wasn't even half an hour into it when a funny little Ford Falcon with a red bubble light on top pulled up in front of the house I was leaving, and a uniformed police officer exited the vehicle.

"I'm gonna need to see some ID," he said as I approached him. I had never heard of the Green River ordinances, something my company's representatives purposely had failed to warn me about. As a result, I had no idea why this officer was stopping me. I was also not worried, at first, because I was unaware I was breaking a local law.

"You know it's against the law to solicit without a permit, don't you?"

"No, Sir, I did not know that."

"Have a seat in the back of the patrol car while I run a check on your ID." I stifled my laugh. The Ford Falcon seemed more like a toy police car than an actual patrol car, but this guy had a gun and a badge and my ID, so it seemed in my best interests to cooperate. I opened the passenger door and flipped the back of the seat forward in order to climb into the back seat where I was able to hear his conversation with his dispatcher. There were no wants or warrants on me, but no permit had been issued in my name either, and I heard the dispatcher tell him to bring me in.

At the police headquarters a desk sergeant informed me I could stipulate to the charge of "soliciting without a permit," a civil forfeiture, and pay a $25.00 fine, or plead not guilty and wait a week for a trial. In today's dollars this would be a fine of $190.00, and I didn't carry that kind of cash around with me. I suggested we go back to my pick-up spot where I could ask my field supervisor for help, but the sergeant just laughed at me.

"When he can't find you, this is where he'll come," and then he ushered me into a cell just as tiny as the Ford Falcon. I did not wait there very long before another Colliers' representative joined me. Boy, were we glad to see each other. We spent our time in lock-up complaining about the company's failure to warn us how this could happen, and also trying to devise an escape plan, just for fun. It was well past our pick-up times when our supervisor finally showed up at the cop shop and regained our freedom by paying our fines. He thought the whole thing was pretty funny, but we did not. He managed to soothe our anger by buying a case of beer.

The next day we made it to Rapid City, South Dakota, where we planned to spend several days before heading into Montana. The first night was uneventful, but the next day was the 4th of July, and our supervisor assured us this afforded our crew an excellent opportunity because families with kids would be at home celebrating with backyard picnics. We all met for breakfast the next morning at the Denny's across the street from our motel, and I noticed I wasn't feeling quite right. I had no appetite, which was very unusual for me. I just ordered coffee and mentioned to my companions it seemed odd not to be hungry. By the time everyone else had finished their food, I felt a little sick to my stomach and light headed. I excused myself and went back to the motel room.

I do not remember much more from the rest of the day, but I do recall when the crew came back at night, they found me naked in the bathroom, delirious, lying on the floor, and hugging the toilet. I'm still thankful to them for getting me dressed and taking me to the hospital emergency room. I was burning up with a fever of 105 degrees. But, of course, I was only eighteen years old, and in those days I could not consent to my own medical treatment. The hospital needed my mother's permission. A nurse dialed my mother's number after finally extracting it from my delirious brain and handed me the phone. By now it was after midnight in Caledonia, and my mom must have been quite worried to get this call.

"Mom, I'm very sick, and you have to tell this nurse it's OK to treat me," I somehow managed to explain and handed the phone back to the nurse. I didn't even try to follow the conversation. My head was swirling and my body was writhing. I remember nothing else. They did manage to bring the fever down some by morning, when the doctor told me I had pneumonia.

How I contracted the pneumonia my doctor was not able to explain. It resulted in a big fork in the road for me, though. I had just finished my senior year of high school as a three-sport athlete in top physical condition. Although I was just 5 feet 9 inches tall and weighed 165 pounds, my plan was to go to the fall tryouts for the freshman football team at the University of Minnesota. Even though I was a decent small-town player, I knew there was not much of a chance for me to make a Big Ten football squad, but I didn't want to regret not trying. Now I wouldn't be able to. When I was finally released from the hospital ten days later, after promising the doctor I would go back to my parent's home and continue to recuperate for a month, I had lost 35 pounds. It would take six months before I regained my strength. The freshman football tryouts would have annihilated me.

So, now I was back in Caledonia. I really didn't mind being there. It's a wonderful place. Some people call it God's country for good reason, with its high hills and deep valleys that somehow escaped the glaciers and were now covered by hardwood forests surrounding rich farmland. I still return three or four times a year, but I just wanted to be in the big city then with all of the grown-up experiences to be had there. Instead, I found myself reduced to spending my days on the couch reading and watching television.

One item in particular caught my eye in *The Winona Daily News* of August 15, one of three newspapers we were getting at the time. A photograph on page three of a young man shaking hands with a priest was captioned, "Pacifist Gets Backing." The headline over the article read, "Gilliam Gets 2-Year Term." According to the article, Robert Gilliam, 22, a recent graduate of St. Mary's College in Winona, received a two-year prison sentence after entering a guilty plea to the charge of refusing induction. "The state wants my body to make war. I am here today because I have refused it. I have refused to cooperate with Selective Service because conscription is a war institution. To cooperate with conscription is to support war," Gilliam told the judge.

You could see this young man was not some hippie/commie/pinko/radical who didn't love this country. He looked like a sincere, intelligent, respectful individual who was taking a moral stand against what was becoming an increasingly questionable military venture by the United States. I had started thinking about this tactic as a response to the war six months earlier when Mohammed Ali had refused induction, but now here was a young man closer in age and circumstances to me, right in my own neighborhood, who had made the same choice. I had to believe these people did not make such a serious decision without considerable reflection about the long-term consequences. I respected the depth of their commitment and knew some soul searching was in store for me.

But I was only eighteen years old, just out of high school, and about to start my university education in a few weeks. I didn't want to go to prison. I knew I would be safe from the draft for four more years with my student deferment. I decided to put off deciding how I would respond to the draft and hope that the war would be over long before I finished school and found myself forced to make a decision. This hope did not allay my guilt, though, and I knew I would have to begin to take some actions against the war. I wrote letters to my senators and congressman and to the editors of the newspapers we read, but I was left feeling inadequate at best. Who pays any real attention to such things? Has any politician ever been swayed by a letter from a constituent, especially one who is too young to vote? Does anyone ever change their mind after reading the op-ed pages? I knew the answer to both questions was "no." I knew in my head and my heart this truth: actions speak louder than words.

19

STOP THE DRAFT WEEK

October 16, 1967
17,544 Dead

I had a by-line article in the *Minnesota Daily* on October 17 appear on page three next to the continuation of the front-page article about local participation in the first National Stop the Draft Week demonstration. According to the article, protesters turned in over 1,000 draft cards across the nation and delivered them to Attorney General Ramsey Clark. Several of the local protesters mentioned by name in the article, David Gutknecht, Fran Shor, and David Pence, would soon be my close friends and comrades when I joined them in the struggle against the war and the draft, but I had not yet met them. Chief Deputy U.S. Marshal James Redpath, also mentioned in the article, would likewise become someone I called a friend even though he arrested me several times over the next two years, but more on that relationship later.

I was anxious to see the paper because I knew I would have my first by-line article. The front-page draft-protest article certainly attracted my attention. I recognized Fran Shor's picture right away, as I had already seen him a few times on campus during impromptu debates that sprang up on the mall and drew sizable crowds on an almost daily basis. His short but somehow still unruly hair and dark rimmed glasses gave him an air of scholar/activist, which he was. It was always possible to hear pro and con points of view on the war with students and even faculty engaging in heated discussions. Fran was an articulate speaker with an impressive ability to recall facts and figures, so his arguments against the war did not rely solely on emotion, which the pro-war speakers did with their "America, love it or leave it" rhetoric. I had seen David Gutknecht once, too, and he impressed me with his quiet solemnity and seriousness of purpose. I read the front-page article on the draft protest and turned to the story's continuation on page three where I first noticed my by-line.

I felt just a tinge of embarrassment (even though there is always a touch of pride to go with a by-line), because my article clearly showed I had spent my time on Monday interviewing 32 girls about their opinions on making Comstock Hall a co-ed dorm. (We did not yet refer to female students as women in 1967. Just like the boys at the University who were under 21, the girls could not vote, sign contracts, or even seek health care without their parents' permission. We were college students living away from home for the first time, but we were legally still classified as children.) Yes, I was assigned by my editor to write this article, but interviewing girls was one of my favorite pastimes anyway. Now I was struck by the seriousness of the protesters and reminded that, while I shared their views, I had not yet done anything substantive to further the cause. These young men were not waiting until they finished school to declare their opposition to conscription. Reading about them definitely accelerated my thinking process. I realized I would have to take some similar action before too long.

A couple of weeks before school started, I returned to Minneapolis and had gone to the *Minnesota Daily* offices in Murphy Hall to introduce myself. The Daily was a completely student-run independent newspaper serving the Twin Cities campus. I'd met The Daily's outgoing senior editor when I won a WCCO-TV journalism scholarship back in February, and he advised me to check in with the paper as soon as I moved to Minneapolis. I found the managing editor and inquired about working for the paper when school started. She said she had a story she wanted covered right away, but she was short staffed for the summer. Could I track down someone in the bursar's office who knew what the status of student fee increases was for the coming school year? I was sure I could. She told me the pay was 35 cents a column inch, 45 cents if I got a by-line. I could check with her every day for assignments, and I could develop a story on my own if I checked first to see if anyone else was already working on it. And just like that, I became a reporter.

This turned out to be the highlight of my university experience. I am now neither proud nor ashamed of the choices I made and the paths I followed, even if some readers will be appalled. (Let me assure you that my individual experience, shaped as it was by my own inner urges, should not be viewed as representative of what the students of the Sixties could and did accomplish at this excellent university. If you set out to be an autodidact, as I did, you are likely to find yourself studying under an inexperienced instructor.) It was, I most fervently believe, my particular learning experience that most certainly led me on the life path toward my wife, the love of my life, and the stepson I cherish. What would I now hold to my heart without them and our friends and the memories we share? All the life I know now would have vanished if I'd changed course back then. I simply accept that I made appropriate choices for the times.

During freshman orientation week before classes started, I met with an adviser assigned to assist me in choosing my classes. She was a good person, well intentioned, and I do not and did not blame her for the disappointment I felt in the schedule we devised. She started out by asking me—please remember she asked me—what class I would most like to take. I said I wanted to take as many courses in creative writing as I could. She told me I could not take any creative writing courses until I finished three trimesters of Freshman English. Okay, then I wanted to take a journalism course right away. Not until I finish two trimesters of Freshman English. But I'm here on a journalism scholarship, and I am already working on the *Minnesota Daily*! Surely such commitment and experience should count for something. But it did not. Then what courses are available to me? My adviser recommended I complete some of the courses required for a liberal arts degree so I could concentrate on my major as an upperclassman. Honestly, I had not really thought much about a degree at this point. I had been more focused on an education, and it never occurred to me these were separate matters.

Consequently, she assigned me, after considerable consternation on my part, Freshman English (five credits), American History (three credits), French Conversation (five credits), and Philosophy/Logic (three credits). I did not choose one single course myself; thus I began my university education under a cloud of skepticism and resentment.

Freshman English was a bust. It may as well have been remedial English. The instructor never looked up from his notes, his desk, or his hands unless he was facing the blackboard, so he never made eye contact with his students. The one thing he stressed the most on the first day of class was we must write our name, course number, section number, and the date in the upper left corner of our papers or he would give the paper an "F" grade without reading it. I guess I did not like being threatened. I had not experienced this level of condescension and ineptitude from a teacher all through my elementary and secondary education, and this was not how I imagined being treated in college. Coupled with how distraught I was with my scheduling debacle, I quickly developed a "Fuck you" attitude toward this instructor and turned in my papers with name, course, section, and date in the upper right corner just to register my heartfelt disaffection. The papers came back to me with a red "F" and the message "See me in my office," without a word and without making eye contact with me even as he handed me the papers himself.

I couldn't take the instructor or the class seriously. I continued to hand in my papers with disdain, although I wrote the assignments with all the skill I could muster in the hopes at some point the instructor would judge the papers on their merits. Then one day while reading in a bathroom stall in the dorm, I realized the dormitory toilet paper, dispensed one folded sheet at a time from a locked box, was so stiff it probably could survive a trip through the typewriter. Voila! My next Freshman English assignment I handed in on toilet paper. This must have been the last straw for the instructor. After he dismissed the class, he addressed me by name.

"Mr. Holland, we need to have a word."

"We do," I agreed as I stepped over to his desk.

"You're failing this course, and you'll have to repeat it if you want a degree."

"I'm not here for a degree. I'm here for an education, and I'm not getting one in any of my classes. You're failing me based on an insignificant procedural point without even reading my papers."

"I'm reading your papers, Mr. Holland, and you should be getting an 'A' in this course, but you're not following the rules. A major facet of a university education is teaching you the importance of following the rules."

"If I should be getting an 'A' then give me an 'A.'"

"But you're not following the rules."

"But it's an incidental, arbitrary rule. Give me a grade commensurate with the work I'm doing."

"If you don't learn to follow the rules while you're in school, you'll be ill-prepared for the real world."

"I'm sick of people telling me the world I'm in isn't real."

We went round and round about the experience, the rules, the future, and I began to see he had struggles of his own as a teaching assistant in a Ph.D. program no longer aligned with what he had imagined for himself when he was a college freshman, so I relinquished my antipathy towards him. We reached an agreement: he would give me a "B" for the course if I did well on the midterm and the final, but I would have to put my name and such in the upper left corner of my remaining papers, a hollow victory for both of us I suppose.

In American History I did not fare much better. This was a lecture series in a hall with seating for a thousand students. The professor walked out on the stage, picked up his microphone, and said, "How many of you are Republicans?" A large number of students raised their hands. "You will receive 'A's," the professor said. "How many of you are Democrats?" Another large number of students raised their hands. "And you will receive 'B's," the professor deadpanned. A lot of students laughed. I did not. Since I had not raised my hand and the professor made no further mention of grades, I figured I had just earned either a "C" or an "F." But I didn't care. This guy was asinine and arrogant, and I never returned for any of his lectures. I showed up for the midterm and the final, received a "B" for the course, and thought, well, I guess he thinks I'm a Democrat.

Philosophy/Logic probably could have been worse, but by the time I arrived in the lecture hall for 500 students, with maybe 150 actually enrolled, it wasn't going to take much to push me over the edge. Out walked the instructor from stage right. She picked up the microphone from her desk, attached it to the placket of her blouse, and meekly, almost inaudibly, introduced herself. Then, just as she turned to write her name on the chalkboard, smoke and sparks began shooting out from the wall where her microphone cord was plugged in. She turned to the class and said, without raising her voice, "Oh, my." A student in the front row quickly stepped forward and yanked the cord out of the wall. This stopped the sparking, but a little column of smoke continued to pour from the opening. I was sitting just three rows from the front, but now, as she continued to lecture without amplification, I couldn't make out what she was talking about, especially when she turned to the blackboard to write her P's and Q's and continued speaking with her back to the class. Sheesh. After the second lecture and the audio system had not been repaired, I quit going to this class. Midterm. Final. C.

My French instructor was cool. She was lively, engaging, and enthusiastic. I did not miss a class. I also did not have a facility for language learning like the fellow who sat next to me did. He was a senior who had completed the required course work for his major in Russian but needed some electives to fill out his credits for graduation. He minored in Italian, so he figured French would be five easy credits, which it was for him. For me it was another C.

Because I was not attending most of my classes, I had a lot of free time on my hands, and I decided to study 20th-century American novelists. I spent countless hours roaming the stacks of the libraries on campus and the Minneapolis Public Library downtown. There were so many novels to read and new writers to discover every day. I read all of the Paris Review "Writers at Work" interviews I could find. As long as the Minnesota autumn weather stayed warm enough, I did much of my reading on Northrop Mall, people watching my fellow students scurrying from class to class.

It wasn't because I grew up a rebel, nor was I trying to be a smart-ass. It's just things were not turning out as I had hoped, and I was trying to make the best of a bad situation by studying novel writing on my own while skipping most of my classes. The friends I had made in the dorm and some of my classes were, by and large, serious students, so I chose not to trouble them with the problems I was having. They could certainly see my face buried in books most of the time and no doubt assumed I was immersed in my coursework.

Spending all my time on the mall also afforded me many opportunities to participate in the frequent spontaneous antiwar discussions that sprang up and drew anywhere from 20 to 200 students, faculty, staff, and whoever else happened to walk by. The war was on everyone's mind. The war was on the television news every night. The war was in all the papers. You could not escape the war in Vietnam in the fall of 1967. Walking around the campus, around Dinkytown, around the West Bank (of the Mississippi River and the Minneapolis campus) also brought me in contact with literature from a wide array of leftist organizations from the Socialist Workers Party to the Twin Cities Draft Information Center, and their papers and pamphlets began to transform my thinking about the war, the government, and our society in general beyond the confines of the tiny town I was from. I was getting an education after all, albeit not a traditional one.

20

"WE ARE MIRED IN A STALEMATE . . ."

February 27, 1968
23,718 Dead

Walter Cronkite owned the title of most trusted man in America. (If you google "most trusted man in America" today, you get both Walter Cronkite and Jon Stewart.) When he returned to New York from an assignment in Vietnam to cover the Tet Offensive and stepped out of his news anchor role to deliver an editorial opinion, millions of Americans took to heart the message he conveyed.

He decried "the terrible loss in American lives, prestige and morale," and the "tragedy of our stubbornness there." He warned us, ". . . for every means we have to escalate, the enemy can match us . . . And with each escalation, the world comes closer to the brink of cosmic disaster."

"To say that we are closer to victory today is to believe, in the face of the evidence, the optimists who have been wrong in the past," he informed us. "To say we are mired in stalemate seems the only realistic, yet unsatisfactory, conclusion."

This was a powerful message coming from the most respected voice in journalism. It had to register with many mainstream Americans. I watched it in the dormitory's common area with a dozen other guys, none of whom I knew very well (very few students had televisions in their rooms in those days), and the reaction in the room was quite solemn. The dormitory was hardly a hotbed of radicalism. In fact, most of the students in this freshman dorm were, like me, from small towns in Minnesota, and we were just finding our way in the big city and the wide, wide world. What resonated in the room was the stark realization that the already disastrous loss of life may have been for naught if there was no possibility of an American victory. Little did we know right then how the death toll would more than double before it was all over.

My conscience beckoned to me again.

21

NORMAN MAILER BACKSTAGE

March 6, 1968
24, 359 Dead

Norman Mailer, one of the most important writers of the time, especially in his own mind, drew a huge, capacity crowd to the Northrop Auditorium on the University campus. The March issue of *Harper's* had just come out, and I devoured his piece, "On the Steps of the Pentagon," an excerpt from his forthcoming book, *Armies of the Night*. Mailer had emerged as one of my favorite living writers during my studies of 20th century American novelists.

I had just finished reading Mailer's novel *Why Are We in Vietnam?* and found it extraordinarily enlightening. Mailer's nonfiction polemics also made for engaging reading, and *Advertisements for Myself, Cannibals and Christians*, and *The Presidential Papers* had all mesmerized me, but with this new novel I experienced an artist exposing America's passion for war in the content of its national character. Reading everything Mailer wrote to that point was more instructive than any of the course work. With the disappointments of my first trimester behind me and the admonishments of my guidance counselor and my parents hanging over me, I now tried my best to regain their confidence in my academic potential by attending all of my classes and completing all of my assignments. But my heart was still not in my university education. I'd expanded my personal studies of 20th century American novelists to include 20th century American poets and was now deeply engaged with Robert Creeley, Charles Olson, William

Carlos Williams, Ezra Pound, and the multitude of poets orbiting their realm. When the opportunity came to see one of the great living writers in person, I was there.

I did have many of the usual college friends, students I had met in the dorm and in my classes, but oddly enough not even one of them could carve out the time to attend Mailer's speech with me, so I went alone. I arrived at Northrop two hours before the scheduled start time because I wanted a good seat. A few hundred students were already lined up in front of the doors before I got there and a few thousand more would soon arrive. I did manage to get a center aisle seat five rows from the front of the stage. I could see the whites of Norman Mailer's eyes from there. I hung on every word as he read for an hour from his soon-to-be published *Armies of the Night*.

When Mailer finished his reading to a standing ovation, he gave a wave to the crowd and exited stage right. As the audience began streaming toward the exit doors at the rear of the auditorium, it occurred to me that the backstage area would be a maze of dressing rooms, storage areas, and passageways where, if I could sneak back there, I just might run into Mailer himself. I had no idea what I might say if I did run into him. I just wanted the chance to see him up close. Security was apparently nonexistent in those days as I slipped unnoticed through the first door leading backstage, and my imaginings about the maze existing there proved remarkably accurate. I guessed Mailer would be heading for an exit to the building where there would be a waiting car, and he had a head start on me. I was moving quickly through the backstage maze when someone called out, "We're over here," and waved me toward where she was standing. She gestured I should enter a tiny, cramped room, which I did. There were already nine people in there. I was ten, and she made eleven. "Norman will be here in a moment," she informed us. "But he only has a few minutes to chat before he has to leave."

I had found the right place. Turned out my compatriots in this little room were the invited members of the English faculty. Now it was common for me in those days to wear a sport coat around campus and to have a week's worth of stubble for a beard, so I suppose I could have passed for an English TA, although I was only 19 and looked it. At any rate, nobody questioned my right to be there. I stood quietly in a corner watching the doorway and not speaking lest my voice give me away.

Norman Mailer entered the room. He greeted each of us, one by one, and asked our names. He took my hand in both of his in a warm and firm embrace. I gave him my name and told him I truly admired his work. He thanked me kindly and moved to the next person, taking her hand in both of his, and then the next, and the next until he had touched everyone in the tiny room, and then he offered to answer any questions we might have.

It is our nature, I imagine, to judge ourselves in comparison to the famous when we encounter them in these informal situations, to search for some flaw in them by which we may deem ourselves at least deserving if not better than they are. Mailer himself provided ample insight into his own failings, so we could use that to tear him down to our own size if we were so inclined. But here in this little room with a dozen people hanging on his every word, I could not detect the arrogance one might have anticipated from him. I wasn't sure if it was his ego or his aura that filled the room, but he filled it with graciousness, patience, insight, and humor. Then he thanked all of us for coming and reminded us we all had a responsibility to do everything we could to bring this war to an end.

This was my call to action. Mailer's speech inspired me but meeting him backstage galvanized my resolve. I now realized it was time for me to join the ranks of those who had already put their lives on the line by trying to stop the war by stopping the draft, including Muhammad Ali, Bob Gilliam, Dave Gutknecht, David Pence, Don Olson, Fran Shor, Sandy Wilkinson, Benjamin Spock, and thousands of other Americans whose moral compass demanded they act on their knowledge of the difference between good and evil. I could no longer believe marching in the street and singing "We Shall Overcome" at the rallies was the most effective way for me personally to stop the killing. I knew in my heart the right and honorable thing to do was to stand up in public and declare, "Hell no! We will not fight this war anymore."

The first thing I decided to do was to inform my girlfriend of my decision. We were the same age and had both left our small town lives to seek our fortunes in the big city. She was not a student but was working as a clerk in a University administrative office. I answered the phone in a friend's dorm room one night, and she was on the other end of the line just calling the freshman dorm exchange to see if she could meet some cool guy. She really did that. We hit it off on the phone, and after ten minutes I gave her my dorm room phone number, went back to my room, and we talked for the rest of the night and every night for two weeks. We had a lot in common: our ages, upbringings, senses of humor. We became very comfortable in our conversation. We became friends. We knew we had to meet, but we were both worried and shared our concern with each other:

what if one of us did not like the other one's looks? We agreed to be honest about it.

It turned out we liked each other's looks just fine and thus began our romance. I am neither proud nor ashamed that I was still a virgin at age nineteen. That's just the way it was. But our passion for each other had brought us to the brink, and I was hopeful she would soon initiate me. Alas, it was not to be.

She was aware of my eagerness to attend every antiwar demonstration on campus, and I knew she was more apolitical than gung-ho on the war, but I anticipated some resistance to the idea of me going to prison for defying the draft. I was right. Don't do it was her attitude. She wouldn't listen to my arguments about the moral responsibilities incumbent on anyone being asked, or forced, to go to war. She told me flat out if I turned in my draft card, she would not see me anymore. It was difficult to do, but I said good-bye and walked away.

Next up I had to tell my family, and I correctly predicted their strenuous objections. Although my mother and stepfather never attended a protest rally themselves, they did not support the war, either. But they certainly did not want their promising young university student with a scholarship going to prison. While I felt I had the moral incumbency argument down pretty well, it was not convincing to a mother's heart. I listened to their objections. I calmly stated my case. The best we could manage was a stalemate.

My next step was probably the most significant one I would take in this whole saga. I was well aware of the Twin Cities Draft Information Center (TCDIC) because they blanketed the U of M campus with informational flyers about their free draft counseling services as well as other antiwar leaflets. I figured it was time for me to pay them a visit to find out what to expect from the legal system once I turned in my draft card. I really didn't know if I would be arrested right away, what to expect about a trial, or what the federal prison system held in store for me, but I expected these guys would know all about such matters, which they did.

When I first walked into the TCDIC offices on Third Avenue just south of downtown, I simply told the receptionist who greeted me I would like to talk with a draft counselor. She told me it would be a short wait as the counselor on duty was in a session at the moment, but I was welcome to browse the literature area while I waited. The office had an impressive array of books and pamphlets, and I was deeply engaged with the reprint of a lengthy Selective Service System memo called "Channeling," which defined the agency's mission as one not only of procuring the necessary military manpower, but also of directing young men into careers deemed important in the war effort. It was chilling. Then I heard a young woman call my name.

Sue Chamberlain invited me into her office, offered me a chair, and asked if I was having a problem with the draft. Yes, I had a problem with the draft. I just couldn't stand by anymore and watch them force the young men of my generation to fight and die in a senseless war. I had decided to send my draft card back to my draft board and just wanted to find out what would happen next. "Oh my," Sue said. "Could you wait just one moment?"

When she returned a few seconds later, she introduced me to Sandy Wilkinson, who shook my hand, invited me to sit down again, and asked if I would mind if Sue sat in on our session. I didn't mind at all. She was in training as a new counselor, and this would be her first time with a new resister. They didn't get people walking in off the street announcing they wanted to resist every day, although it did happen from time to time.

Sandy was a resister and one of the co-founders of TCDIC. With his short-cropped dark hair, neat clothes, and calm demeanor, he quickly made me feel at ease. He was very knowledgeable about what I could expect. First of all, though, he wanted to talk about how I had come to my decision. I went through my process in detail, starting with reading about the two soldiers killed in Vietnam when I was ten years old. We shared our personal stories over the next couple of hours. Sandy was a couple of years older than me and had experience as a young college student working on voter registration drives in the south. He shared some harrowing stories of being threatened by local sheriffs. He had turned in his draft card the previous October during the first National Stop the Draft Week. I told him I remembered reading about him in the paper. We talked about Martin Luther King, Gandhi, Thoreau, and nonviolent civil disobedience movements in general. Here was someone, for the first time in my young life, with similar thoughts and feelings to my own, in contrast to my college friends who were good people opposed to the war but not interested in making personal sacrifices to back up their opposition.

Sandy explained the process I could expect to unfold after returning my draft card to my local draft board. First, the draft board would revoke my student deferment and reclassify me 1-A Delinquent, which would put me at the top of the local board's list for induction, ahead even of the volunteers. I would then have thirty days to appeal my reclassification by requesting a personal appearance. After the appearance, the board would issue an induction notice within one to three months. Indictments typically followed six months to a year after refusing induction. It could take three to six months for a trial to take place. Sentencing might be two or three months after the trial. Draft resisters were usually granted bail while they appealed convictions, and those appeals could take six months or more. In all it could be a year and a half to two years, maybe more, before I saw the inside of a prison cell. This was a relief to me as I had imagined "justice" would be much swifter.

At the conclusion of our lengthy, informative, and engaging meeting, Sandy gave me the phone number for Chester Bruvold, a local attorney who was handling many of the local draft cases in court. Sandy thought Chester could give me a more detailed explanation of the legal processes and another perspective before I fully committed myself to action. I appreciated this and called Chester at his office as soon as I returned to my room. He suggested I meet him at his home that evening, where he took me into his basement woodworking shop for our tête-à-tête. I enjoyed sitting on a stool surrounded by all of his woodworking tools while he meticulously cleaned his tobacco pipe. His calm and direct manner relaxed me as we delved again into the calamity of the war and the urgency to end it. Even as Chester laid out the seriousness of the life-changing consequences ahead of me, I felt relieved to know a man of his stature was there to advise me.

The next day I met again with Sandy, and he introduced me to Dave Gutknecht. This was like meeting a celebrity. I had read about Dave a number of times in the local press and had seen him deliver a speech in front of a large crowd. Meeting him in person like this I was impressed with his calm and gentle nature, but over time I would learn there was no more dedicated and committed opponent to the war and the draft than Dave. The three of us talked about my meeting with Chester, and then Sandy mentioned a demonstration was being planned at which a friend of theirs would be turning in his draft card and perhaps I would want to be a part of the event. I loved the idea. At this point, all I had imagined was I would write a letter to my draft board on the typewriter in my room and then drop it in the mailbox with my draft card enclosed. But to make a public proclamation with press coverage seemed like the proper thing to do. People needed to know there were young men of conscience willing to risk their own well-being to steer the country away from its current descent into madness.

Later I would realize I was being vetted in these first sessions as the group did not want just any freak off the street who might be seeking personal notoriety rather than focusing on the common good. I am proud to say I passed the test. I also realized later I was evaluating TCDIC as an organization I might affiliate with, and they passed with flying colors as well. I ended up working full time and living with these people for the next two years.

22

MLK Assassinated

April 4, 1968
25,773 Dead

An unbearable tragedy unfolded on May 4, 1968 as Dr. Martin Luther King, Jr., the hero of the nonviolent protest movement, was gunned down in the prime of his life. More and more the world was spinning out of control around me. Dr. King had become one of the most important and influential thinkers in my development as a political person, and I was shattered by this event. A wave of fear, anger, and anguish stunned the nation.

It is difficult to explain the emotions of this time. The hatred on both sides was palpable, from the racists within our nation who applauded King's death to those of us heartbroken, devastated, inconsolable, and filled with hate for the people who could even countenance such a crime against humanity.

One year to the day prior to his assassination, Dr. King had delivered one of his most important speeches, "A Time to Break Silence," at the Riverside Church in New York City. Against the advice of his closest advisers, who saw King's opposition to the war as a growing distraction from the civil rights movement, he assured his listeners of his complete agreement with the recent statement issued by Clergy and Laymen Concerned about Vietnam: "A time comes when silence is betrayal." In Vietnam, King said, "that time has come for us."

Understanding the enormity of his mission for civil rights in America and the danger to his cause that speaking out against the government, and especially against President Johnson, would entail simply underscored the dire circumstances dragging the country ever deeper into the abyss of war. If ever my own commitment wavered, which it did not, Dr. King's death strengthened my resolve.

The assassin silenced the voice but not the man, as his words and spirit live on even today.

23

PARIS PEACE TALKS BEGIN

May 11, 1968
28,196 Dead

While I certainly hoped peace would result from the Paris talks, there was still too much war going on for me to step back from my plans to publicly join the resistance. In fact, the negotiations over the next eight months would result in one decision in Paris: the shape of the conference table. At this pace, one could not imagine the fighting would ever end. The responsibility to stop the war still remained on the shoulders of the young men being compelled to fight it.

Of course my mother and stepfather and my friends took the announcement of peace talks as a sign I should delay my plans to publicly declare my resistance. I understood it was difficult for them to see past the prison walls which would soon confine me, but I tried my best to explain that even if a rapid conclusion of the war miraculously occurred, which was not likely, the draft itself remained a menace because it enabled the government to repeat this mistake in some new theater of operations over and over again.

I often argued that the government would not be able to raise an all-volunteer force of the size used in Vietnam. Some people touted the large number of enlistments during Vietnam as proof of support for the war effort, but enlistment was a popular strategy for avoiding deployment to Vietnam. Deals could be made with recruiters to secure noncombat deployments, even though recruits did not always realize, until it was too late, these deals did not have to be honored by the military. (For an enlightening perspective on this issue, you could read R.M. Ryan's autobiographical novel, *There's a Man with a Gun Over There.*) Statistics available from the Department of Defense show enlisted men, not draftees, committed over half of the 507,000 incidents of desertion recorded during the Vietnam War.

I also pointed out all of the lies we had been listening to about the "light at the end of the tunnel" for years on end. No, I told my family and friends, peace is not at hand, the draft still must be abolished, and I will proceed as planned.

24

GOODBYE, MY DRAFT CARD

May 20, 1968
28,873 Dead

I felt very alive as I climbed into the passenger seat of Sandy's car for the drive to downtown St. Paul, where we would stage a demonstration in front of the Federal Building in support of the Boston Five, whose trial on conspiracy charges began that very day. The five—who were indicted for "conspiring to counsel, aid, and abet" violations of the Selective Service laws—were the already very famous Dr. Benjamin Spock; Yale Chaplin William Sloane Coffin; author Mitchell Goodman; Institute for Policy Studies founder Marcus Raskin; and Harvard graduate student Michael Ferber. Their manifesto, "A Call to Resist Illegitimate Authority," had been published in *The New York Review of Books* and was signed by over 300 prominent university professors and writers. Certainly the government hoped to stifle such organized public opposition to the war by indicting as co-conspirators these five men and "others known and not known," but the prestige of these professionals brought instead a measure of mainstream legitimacy. It was my intent to honor them by answering their call to resist.

We planned our demonstration for noon so we could attract the lunch crowd. Leaflets in support of The Boston Five, which also announced I would return my draft card to my draft board during the demonstration, were distributed to passersby. We drew a crowd just shy of a hundred supporters and curious onlookers. Sandy made a speech in support of The Boston Five, and then I read my letter to the draft board informing them I would no longer participate in the killing machine. I called on the members of the draft board to join me by shutting down the Caledonia board and refusing to send any more young men from our town to Vietnam. I held my draft card up for the crowd to see, placed it inside the letter, slipped the letter into the stamped envelope, licked and sealed it, and walked to the corner where I put it in a mailbox.

There were some cheers and a few boos. That was to be expected. While opposition to the war was steadily increasing, there remained a solid base of support for the war, especially from those who bought into the government's scare tactics, which focused on cultivating fear of world domination by the communists. Our corps of organizers stayed on the federal plaza for an hour after the speeches to pass out leaflets and engage in conversation and debate. I deemed it a successful act of civil disobedience, and for the first time in my first year away from home I felt as though I had done something that could have an impact on our nation's future.

We all drove back to the TCDIC offices, and that is where and when my real education began. The draft resistance movement consisted of individuals from varied backgrounds who all came to the decision to resist from their own deeply held personal moral codes. We had Jews, Catholics, Protestants, atheists, agnostics, hippies, pagans, Buddhists, and more. Those with any and all philosophical beliefs were welcome. There was no pressure to adopt a particular political persuasion either, but I quickly found if I wanted to follow the conversation I needed to read Marx, Mao, Trotsky, Bakunin, Chomsky, Zinn, Goodman, and many more writers and thinkers whose works became crucial to my evolution as a political being. Most of these books and essays were available in the TCDIC offices, and I spent the summer devouring new knowledge and perspective. This course of study and the ensuing discussions with my compatriots brought me fully to the belief that revolutionary change in the structure of our society was not only necessary but close at hand.

Many of the other antiwar groups of the time had more dogmatic philosophies or even restrictive membership policies. No need to single them out by name here; we all know they existed. But each group reached their core constituency, resulting in an overall sense of community and shared purpose: we all opposed the war.

I also wanted to feel more effective on a day-to-day basis, so I immersed myself in TCDIC's training to become a draft counselor. Sandy was the "lead" or "head draft counselor." Although we did not generally use titles denoting a hierarchy within the organization, and we had no top-down

George Crocker holds the microphone as I read my Refusal Statement to supporters at my induction refusal. Photo by Zerby from the *Minneapolis Star-Tribune*. Courtesy of the Minnesota Historical Society

chain of command, people did assume leadership roles for specific tasks as dictated by their particular skill sets and experience. Hence, Sandy facilitated the counselor training. Step one was to read and study the Selective Service Rules and Regulations, which were published in an encyclopedia-sized set of volumes. Step two was to sit in on counseling sessions with Sandy and other experienced counselors. We also had meetings with movement lawyers who were working on legal and constitutional challenges through the courts. They gave us insights into mistakes made by draft boards during their legal work.

By the end of the summer I considered myself a crackerjack counselor. I became adept at finding loopholes in the law and draft board errors that enabled me to restore lost deferments and delay for months on end impending induction notices. Each small victory felt like a potential life saved. The draft boards were made up of volunteer community members who were basically rubber stamps for the full-time paid clerks who wielded the real power. But the clerks found it difficult to run their operations "by the book" because "the book" was a seventeen-volume encyclopedic set of rules and regulations they were not nearly as well trained in as we were. Mistakes were rampant, and we were happy to take advantage of them.

While I immersed myself in these activities for the summer, I also need-ed to find a job in order to pay my share of the rent on the two-bedroom apartment I was sharing with three of my dorm buddies. Good old-fash-ioned newspaper want ads led me to a "houseman position" at a downtown hotel where a man twice my age taught me how to set up banquet rooms and where to hide liquor bottles so we could sneak break-time nips. The job was within walking distance of my apartment, though still a hike. The second-shift hours suited me just fine. I reported for duty at 3:00 p.m. and finished at 11:00 p.m., which gave me the opportunity to leaflet the induc-tion center at 6:30 in the morning and then spend half a day at TCDIC studying, learning, and doing draft resistance work.

25

RFK Assassinated

June 5, 1968
29,878 Dead

What am I living in, the fucking Dark Ages? I could not take any more tragedy. I could not comprehend the insanity. I was just nineteen years old, but in the last five years I had witnessed five major political assassinations: Medgar Evers, John F. Kennedy, Malcolm X, Dr. Martin Luther King, Jr., and now Robert F. Kennedy. How could this be considered a reasonable method for the resolution of disputes? How could this lead to anything but chaos? There were no answers to these questions in the books I was reading or the discussions in which I participated. The only answer I could manage was to steel my resolve regarding nonviolence as the essential component in fostering change.

Minnesota's own Senator Eugene McCarthy had declared his intention to run against his party's incumbent president way back on November 30, 1967, saying, "I am concerned that the Administration seems to have set no limit to the price it is willing to pay for a military victory." McCarthy was primarily responsible for driving Johnson out of the race when he tallied 42% of the New Hampshire primary votes to Johnson's 49%, highlighting the increasing divide within the Democratic Party over the Vietnam War. But Kennedy's entry in the race immediately split the antiwar faction in two. Kennedy had the youth and charisma and national name recognition McCarthy lacked, so he drew many college age activists into his campaign. Once Johnson dropped out of the race, Minnesota's former senator and now Vice President, Hubert Humphrey, entered the fray with the immediate support of the party's establishment.

These were wild times. Here was an incumbent president bowing out of an election because he could not extricate himself from a war he was unable to win. The two antiwar candidates garnered a combined 80% of the primary votes, but Humphrey, who entered the race too late to qualify for the primaries, compiled his delegates from caucus states controlled by party leaders and easily won the nomination on the first ballot. But the real story of this convention took place in the streets of Chicago where antiwar protesters were attacked, tear gassed, and beaten by police. While eight of the protesters, who numbered in the thousands, were later indicted on charges of "conspiracy to incite a riot," a government-appointed commission of 200 members released the Walker Report in December of 1968 in which they characterized the convention violence as a "police riot." I remember watching night after night as the protesters chanted, "The whole world is watching," while they were being beaten, arrested, and dragged away. Once again, television brought the spectacle into the living rooms of America

The Walker Report stated that the " . . . response was unrestrained and indiscriminate police violence on many occasions . . . made all the more shocking by the fact that it was often inflicted upon persons who had broken no law, disobeyed no order, made no threat. These included peaceful demonstrators, onlookers, and large numbers of residents who were simply passing through, or happened to live in, the areas where confrontations were occurring."

Despite these findings, the federal grand jury, now under control of Richard Nixon's Attorney General, John Mitchell, ignored the recommendation of Ramsey Clark, the preceding Attorney General who had instituted the investigation, and issued the conspiracy charges against the demonstration's leaders, the Chicago Eight, in March of 1969.

A circus trial followed which was both appalling and repulsive to watch because of the despicable courtroom decorum displayed by the now infamous Judge Julius Hoffman. His inappropriate conduct and obvious bias against the defendants resulted in reversals of all the convictions, including his multiple citations for contempt of court against all the defendants and their attorneys.

Could the convention have turned out differently, and might the course of the war been drastically altered had Robert Kennedy not been assassinated? There is, of course, no way to know.

26

Hello George Wallace

July 4, 1968
31,036 Dead

I had to pee. There was a certain urgency to this need. I was in the middle of downtown Minneapolis, and it was bad form in those days to just walk into a restaurant and use their restroom. People were always on the lookout for hippies and homeless people who might, God forbid, pee in their toilet. But I knew my way around my city pretty well. I knew I just had to run up Hennepin Avenue a couple of blocks to the corner of 7th Street where there was a public restroom in a hallway between the parking garage and the Radisson Hotel. You could access this facility from the hotel lobby, from the garage, or from a narrow almost-hidden passageway right off 7th Street most people didn't even know about. These three entrances all converged at the restroom door in a tiny anteroom. When I got to the corner of 7th and Hennepin, I couldn't get across the street because the light was against me and the traffic was heavy, so I moved toward the Radisson on the opposite side of the street looking for an opening in the traffic. I spotted my chance and dashed across the street, dodging a car, leaping over a fire hydrant, and entering the narrow passageway at a full speed run. Just as I entered the anteroom, with relief in sight, three guys in suits grabbed me, twisted my arms behind my back, and threw me against the wall.

Somebody's hand was pressing my face hard against the wall forcing my eyes to look right at the door from the parking garage, and just then George Wallace came striding through, flanked by four more men in suits and looking straight ahead as he walked through the hallway, as if nothing at all was going on there. The three guys in suits who had grabbed me were part of Wallace's security entourage, of course, which I did not know when they grabbed me. They frisked me for weapons and one of them asked me, "Where're you running to so fast?"

"I gotta pee," I told him. "I really, really have to pee," and I pointed at the restroom door.

"Check it out," the talking suit said to one of the other suits, who peaked in and reported it was empty with no window. "Go ahead and pee," he said to me, "and then come right back out here."

"Ahhhhhh!" Then I washed my hands. Then I washed my face. Then I took a deep breath and went back out to see what the goon squad had planned for me, but they were gone.

Later in the afternoon I returned to the apartment hoping to share my experience with some of my college buddies. As I opened the door a distraught Rob, who was literally wringing his hands, immediately accosted me.

"Danny, I've done something terrible."

"What now, Rob," I said calmly while checking through the mail. Rob was always doing something terrible, although it could also be quite funny, like the time his girlfriend broke up with him. He got drunk and somehow managed to climb up on the marquee of the Varsity Theater in Dinkytown and rearranged the letters from the movie title to say, "Fuck Linda." And he didn't get caught doing it.

"I stole a car," he said through labored, agitated breaths.

"You what!? Why would you do that?"

"I was just walking along the river, down by the steam plant, and I saw this car with a George Wallace bumper sticker, and it made me so mad, and then I noticed the keys were in it, and the window was open, so I just got in and drove away to, you know, teach the guy a lesson."

"Please tell me you're kidding."

"No. I stole a car."

"Rob, Rob, Rob. Where is the car now?"

He walked over to the front window and pointed across the street. "Right there. The gold and white Fairlane with the open window. What am I going to do?"

"Nothing," I said. "Just leave it there and the police will find it."

"What about these keys?" Rob asked and showed me a key ring with at least a dozen keys on it.

I grabbed the keys out of his hand and said, "Listen, Rob, I have to go over to TCDIC, and I won't be back until late, so I am going to toss these keys in the open window of the car. When the cops find the car, the owner will have his car and his keys back. You've done a very bad thing, Rob, and you could go to jail for this. I want you to promise me you will not go near the car again. Do you understand me?"

"Yes. I know. You're right."

I realize now I probably should have called the police and told them where the car was, but at the time I was afraid they would somehow trace the call or track us down and Rob would still get in trouble. But Rob had no impulse control. His guilt got the better of him, and when it got dark and the car was still there, he decided to drive it back down to the steam plant where he found it. He wrote a note explaining why he took the car and apologizing to the owner, slipped it in the visor, and headed down to the river. He only got a few blocks from the apartment when he saw the flashing red lights of a police cruiser behind him. When the police officer casually walked up to the driver's side window, Rob just handed him the note. After reading the note, the officer laughed and said, "This is funny because we just pulled you over to tell you to turn on your headlights. But now you're going to have to step out of the car. You're under arrest." Rob managed to avoid any jail time, but he had to pay a stiff fine, he was put on probation, and he was expelled from the University.

Not even someone who advocated civil disobedience, as I did, would condone stealing a car as a way to teach someone a lesson over a bumper sticker. But if you had been around in 1968 and heard the vile, racist rhetoric of George Wallace, e.g., "In the name of the greatest people that have ever trod this earth, I draw a line in the dust and toss the gauntlet before the feet of tyranny, and I say, segregation now, segregation tomorrow and segregation forever," who knows what you might have done.

27

HELL NO!

September 23, 1968
34,107 Dead

Mulford Q. Sibley, long time peace activist and political science professor at the University of Minnesota, honored me with his support, and my heart felt warmed by upwards of 100 people dedicated enough to appear at a 6:30 a.m. antiwar demonstration. George Crocker came decked out in his Uncle Sam suit and manned the bullhorn for Sibley while he addressed the crowd from the front steps of the Old Federal Building, then serving as the induction center. A photograph of the two of them landed right smack dab in the middle of the front page of the *Minneapolis Tribune* the next morning.

As predicted by me and thousands of other prognosticators, there had been no discernible progress in the Paris Peace Talks while the casualties climbed relentlessly. Sibley quoted from a letter to a Russian youth by Leo Tolstoy: "In every person's life there are moments in which he can know himself, tell himself who he is, whether he is a man who values his human dignity above his life." I told the crowd this was certainly such a moment for me, and a feeling of freedom overwhelmed me.

"The government may put my body behind bars for refusing induction today, but it will never control my conscience. It is people of conscience who will bring this war to an end, so I will go inside this building right now and tell the army, 'Hell no!'" Then I turned and entered the induction center through its revolving door.

Once inside the building I was completely on my own. It was me against them. My order to report for induction included a second-floor room number. I climbed the stairs, found the designated room, and joined my fellow inductees. Most of the thirty-some men were sitting quietly in the standard classroom desk-chairs, but a few pairs, buddies probably, were standing in the back talking with each other. I addressed the room.

"Good morning, my fellow conscripts. Today is not going to proceed exactly as you may have thought it would. When the duty officer reports to this room in the next couple of minutes to induct us into the army, I'm going to say 'Hell No.' If any of you have doubts or misgivings about entering the army, you can certainly join me. You can always come back tomorrow or next week or next month, and they will still let you join the army. But if you go into the army today and change your mind tomorrow or next week or next month, they will not let you leave."

Not one of the conscripts said a word in response. I was going to continue with more thoughts on the war and the draft when a sergeant and a lieutenant entered the room.

"Everybody take a seat," the sergeant ordered and the handful of men at the back of the room found their chairs. I remained standing at the front of the room just a few feet from the two men in uniform.

"Sit down," the sergeant commanded, pointing to an empty chair in the front row.

"Hell No!" I replied. "Let's stop the killing now."

Not everyone who refused induction went right into the room where the ceremony took place in order to make their refusal known. In fact, our movement lawyers cautioned me against it as the army might try to take jurisdiction of the case. The induction process was very brief. I was advised the duty officer would tell the inductees to stand and take one step forward, and then he would administer an oath of allegiance. The army considered you "in" when you took the step forward. Refusing the oath would get you arrested on the spot, thrown in a military brig, and court-martialed. Still, I felt strongly the proper way to refuse induction was to do so in the presence of my fellow inductees, to make it clear they had other choices as well. But I did not want to follow any order or instruction from these military men, such as "Sit down," lest they think I accepted their authority over me, so I must be in the army.

"You must be the reason all those people are out in front of the building this morning," the lieutenant surmised.

"That is correct," I replied.

"May I ask your name, so I can check it off my list here and indicate you are refusing to be inducted."

"Daniel Holland. Proudly refusing induction."

"If you wouldn't mind, I'd like to meet with you in my office for a minute to formalize your refusal."

I had not anticipated being invited to an office for any formalities, but I wanted to see where he was going with this. When we sat down together at his desk, just the two of us, he pulled out a blank sheet of paper and asked me if I would write out my refusal to be inducted. I handed him my two-page, single-spaced induction refusal statement, and told him I would not write it out again.

"Will you sign your typed statement?" he asked.

"Of course." I signed it, as big as John Hancock, and the lieutenant signed, dated, and noted he had received it from me.

"Your statement may appear as evidence against you in a court of law," he advised me.

"Oh, I hope it is," I informed him.

"It is my duty to offer you one last chance here to obey this lawful order for induction. If you stand up now and take one step forward, I will administer the oath of allegiance, and we can throw this statement of yours in the trash." He shook the papers I had given him and held them over the wastebasket next to his desk.

"You have to be joking. Right?" I fretted.

"No. It is my duty to make the offer. But I accept your refusal." He stood up and with his outstretched hand indicated the open door to his office. "We both have busy days ahead of us now."

"Let's get to it," I said, and left.

The crowd outside gave me a rousing cheer as I exited the building. I spoke some more with them about what I had experienced inside. We sang some protest songs. By then it was 8:00 a.m. and time to tackle the day's chores. My supporters included students, working people, and activists, all of whom had responsibilities to attend to.

At this moment of my life, I was still registered as a student at the University of Minnesota, and the press would refer to me as a College of Liberal Arts student at the University who had just refused induction even though he could have stayed out of the draft with a student deferment. But I had not been going to any of my classes, as I was completely caught up in my studies and work with the Twin Cities Draft Information Center, so I decided to formally withdraw from the University. I might have just walked away without a word, but because I was attending school on a full tuition scholarship from WCCO Television, which had already paid for the semester, I wanted to withdraw from school before the deadline, so WCCO would receive a refund they might apply to future scholarship recipients.

When the fall semester started, my college buddies moved back to the dorm, and I had to leave the apartment we'd had for the summer. With no particular place to go, I ended up on the couch at the house occupied by David Pence, Dan Miler, and Charlie Christianson on University Avenue. David and Dan were full-time staff members at TCDIC committed to organizing antiwar activities in the high schools. Charlie was a generation ahead of us, I think he was pushing forty, and worked full time as a firefighter with the Minneapolis Fire Department. He was also a longtime activist and one of the most fiery and eloquent public speakers on the protest scene. Sleeping on their couch and just being in their midst contributed greatly to my continuing education as an antiwar advocate.

Very soon after I refused induction, I was invited to become the next full-time staff member of TCDIC, and I don't mind saying I was more honored by this vote of confidence than by any previous accolades. This was acknowledgment by my peers that I had arrived at a suitable level of commitment and experience, and my continuing contributions to our cause were expected and respected. TCDIC had attained a level of national recognition as a significant player in the draft resistance movement, with a high number of public resisters, a solidly staffed office for draft counseling, continual daily leafleting at and disruption of the induction center, and community outreach programs providing antiwar speakers to schools, churches, clubs, and any group or organization seeking a peaceful alternative to American military aggression. We published a monthly newsletter with over 1,500 subscribers, and distributed thousands of pieces of antiwar and anti-draft literature every month. Our full-time paid (subsistence level of $80 per month) staff hovered around 15 or 16 people who each put in 60-plus hours per week. Organizers recruited supporters to show up at 6:30 in the morning whenever we knew someone would refuse induction and also to show up in court not just for trials but for preliminary hearings and sentencing as well. We also met regularly with other antiwar groups in the Twin Cities coordinating activities and cosponsoring some of the largest protest demonstrations in Minnesota's history.

TCDIC had emerged from the 1967 Vietnam Summer project in the Twin Cities, which focused on educational work against the war and the draft in the off-campus community. Founders Sandy Wilkinson, Tom Smit, and Dave Gutknecht, who all became public resisters, rented a small office on Fourth Avenue just south of downtown Minneapolis and raised operating funds through small contributions and fundraisers. Word-of-mouth was the closest thing to the Internet back then, and it proved to be a valuable tool in spreading the news that TCDIC offered free (donations accepted) draft counseling. While resistance was a core component of the organization's philosophy, young men seeking advice learned about all of their options and the attendant consequences available to them from emigration to Canada, conscientious objector (CO) status, medical, student, fatherhood, or other deferments, and resistance without pressure to choose any particular path.

In late October 1967, Dave Gutknecht received a telephoned bomb threat at the TCDIC offices, and later the same night, when no one was there, a small incendiary device crashed through the front window. The landlord evicted the group, so they moved two blocks away to Third Avenue South where they operated for nearly a year before another firebombing and eviction. The third and final office of TCDIC's five-year life was on the corner of 6th Street and Cedar Avenue.

Group decisions were made by consensus or general agreement, not by any leadership structure. Once you were invited to become a full-time, paid staff member, you were expected to produce results. Biweekly staff meetings, which could go on for many hours, included individual reports on each person's activities. Disagreements might arise about tactics or direction, but these would be resolved through discussion and compromise.

Certainly there were people I looked to for guidance, people whose opinions and motives I trusted. I considered Dave Gutknecht and Sandy Wilkinson mentors due to their extensive experience, and both men possessed a calm and thoughtful demeanor that exuded confidence. David Pence was more flamboyant with a rousing public persona. He could fire up any crowd and had an unending store of knowledge on history and political issues. Doug Gutknecht, Dave's brother, who managed the organization's finances, was one of the smartest people I ever met, as was Mary Gutknecht, their sister. Scott Alarik became my best friend. I was quite impressed by this seventeen-year-old who had already made the commitment to refuse to register for the draft. George Crocker possessed one of the quietest personalities I ever encountered, but also one of the most powerful because he embodied the very definition of sincerity. Curly haired and enthusiastic, Don Olson was the epitome of the tireless organizer. (Many more people were important to my evolution as an activist. I am afraid I would miss too many of them if I tried to list all of them here, so I have mentioned every name I could remember in the acknowledgments.)

Another event of momentous consequence for me occurred soon after I refused induction. This was our establishment of a resistance commune, which became known as Colfax House because of its location at 26th Street and Colfax Avenue South. Jim and Maryann Grage, longtime supporters of TCDIC and committed activists from the University community, answered our call for help in finding a house for resistance workers by putting a down payment on a triplex, which we took over completely; each of us who moved in paid, I think, $17 a month to cover the mortgage. I remember eleven of us moved in initially, and everyone had his or her own bedroom unless they wanted to share. During the year I lived there, some people moved on and new people moved in so somewhere around 30-plus people made Colfax House their home at one time or another.

As might be expected with such a large group, some conflicts arose. I remember a brouhaha erupted over dirty dishes that required a house meeting to resolve. The ensuing discussion revealed we were never having meals together as a group. Rick Sklader, our resident Marxist, took up the gauntlet and challenged all of us by holding high his copy of *Quotations from Chairman Mao* (Little Red Book) and exhorting us to action, asking, "Where do community dinners come from? Do they fall from the sky like manna from heaven? No! They must be organized!" And with undaunted resolve he formed committees for cooking, shopping, and cleanup. The resulting dinner was more than just successful. After a few rewarding community meals together, we decided to share the experience with the other resistance commune, Harriet House. Dinner for 30 then blossomed into community-wide potluck dinners that became a staple at St. Stephens church and drew over 200 people every Monday night from many of the area's activist organizations.

Now I was living and working, eating and breathing the resistance. The intoxicating feelings of revolutionary fervor infected our waking and sleeping lives with our commitment and dedication to ending the war, eliminating the draft, changing the country, and saving the world.

28

Milwaukee 14 Action

September 24, 1968
34,147 Dead

As I mentioned earlier, something dramatic happened almost every day in the Sixties. Surprise, surprise, the very next day after I refused induction in Minneapolis, a group of fourteen activists in a daring daylight raid struck the offices of the Milwaukee draft boards.

Of course, the only people who knew the Milwaukee 14 action was going to take place were the 14 men who carried it out and one or two support personnel who brought the press to witness the action. Even though Fred Ojile and Doug Marvy were active in TCDIC and good friends, and Father Al Janicke was well known to us, they could not jeopardize the mission by telling us ahead of time they were going to act. We were all surprised when word came in about our three friends from Minneapolis who had joined eleven other activists in a raid on the Milwaukee draft boards, destroying over 10,000 files by burning them with homemade napalm in a small park in front of the Brumder Building (now the Germania Building) in downtown Milwaukee.

The Milwaukee 14 joined a growing protest movement that became known as the ultra-resistance. The Big Lake One, the Baltimore Four, the Catonsville Nine, and the Boston Two preceded them. The Pasadena Three, the Silver Spring Three, the Chicago Fifteen, Women Against Daddy Warbucks, the New York Eight, the D.C. Nine, the Beaver 55, and over 300 additional raids on draft boards, corporate headquarters, and FBI offices followed. Many of these activists were well past draft age or exempt from the draft because of their status as clergy, but they wanted to show their solidarity with the young men risking prison by defying the draft. This is why most of these actions were referred to as "hit and stay," meaning the participants waited at the scene for the police to arrest them in order to present in court their views on the illegality and immorality of the war. As time went on, more and more of these actions would be "hit and run," as the participants believed they could more effectively disrupt the draft by committing multiple actions, so they did not stay at the scene and wait for arrest.

Having three of our own involved in a major event that received international attention certainly brought the matter home for us. Sides quickly formed for and against taking such actions. Some argued that destruction of property was a violent act and therefore had no place in a movement built on the ideals of peaceful protest, nonviolence, and noncooperation. Others believed some property, like draft files, only existed to further the violence of the war and must be destroyed in order to protect the innocent. I tended to agree with the side in support of file burning or destruction. I could not see any value inherent in a piece of paper used to identify a specific man and order him into battle. I could not, in good conscience, support damaging or bombing a building, or blowing up a car. Some activists also destroyed the office typewriters used to create the files, but I did not support that because the typewriter had inherent value and could be turned to peaceful purposes. Then people started damaging just the "1" and the "A" keys so the typewriters could not be used to create "1-A" draft cards, which were sent to those who were first in line to be drafted. This was primarily a symbolic gesture.

The transcendent symbolism of the Milwaukee 14 action, though, appeared in the photo seen all over the world of fourteen men gathered around a raging fire in the middle of a downtown street linked arm in arm and singing hymns while waiting for the police to arrive and arrest them. The vision of these men in front of the fire spoke volumes about their commitment by saying we are risking our lives and our futures to do whatever we can to stop an illegal and immoral war. This was a symbol meant to inspire the conscience of the country. This was a call to action.

29

Honeywell Project

December 8, 1968
36,388 Dead

What an honor to have known Marv Davidov, one of the kindest and most dedicated advocates for peace to grace our planet. Shortly after we moved the TCDIC offices into the second floor space on Cedar Avenue, Marv rented the first floor of the building and set up his Liberty House outlet, offering to the community handcrafted products made by former farm laborers, sharecroppers, and domestics trying to keep their traditional crafts and ethnic styles alive.

I loved stopping into Marv's space on my way out after work or even for a lunch break in the storefront. Marv was seventeen years my senior, and he had more stories to tell than I could begin to imagine. It was inspirational to make friends with someone who had been at the forefront of the struggle for civil rights and peace longer than I had been living.

Marv was one of just seven white people from Minnesota who had been on the Freedom Rides in the early Sixties. He was arrested in Jackson, Mississippi, in 1961 when his contingent arrived at the Greyhound Bus depot in Jackson and the white Freedom Riders tried to order lunch in the "Negro" waiting area. A recent Supreme Court ruling had prohibited discrimination on the basis of race at interstate travel facilities. The Freedom Riders were trying to make the law apply in real life situations. Instead they were severely beaten or arrested.

After Marv and his group were arrested, they were able to meet briefly with a black attorney who told them, "Negroes don't serve on juries in Mississippi, and neither do women, Catholics, or Jews. It will take about fifteen minutes for the all-male, white, Baptist jury to convict you." Sure enough, he was right. They were all sentenced to four months in prison. While "Jail not bail" had been their rallying cry, they had been advised they would lose their right to appeal their convictions if they stayed in jail more than thirty-nine days. On day thirty-nine they posted bail and filed an appeal. Frank Sinatra, Ella Fitzgerald, and other celebrities had raised the bail money for the Freedom Riders.

Stories like this were intoxicating, and Marv seemed to have a never-ending supply of them. But he was not stuck in the past. Marv had recently returned to Minneapolis from a stint on the West Coast working with the War Resisters League when an editorial by Staughton Lynd in *Liberation* magazine captured his attention. Lynd proposed the protest movement carry out sustained campaigns against corporate weapons producers.

Marv did not have to look far to find the perfect target in Honeywell, Inc., Minnesota's largest military contractor. Honeywell was deeply involved in the manufacture of antipersonnel fragmentation bombs. These devastating devices were delivered via cluster bombs containing upwards of 600 or more bomblets about the size of a baseball with each one containing its own detonator. Every bomblet was studded with BB's that scattered at very high velocity in all directions when the bomblet detonated. Protruding from the surface of the bomblets were spirals of sharpened steel winglets to aid in their wide area coverage and add to the deadly fragmentation. Tens of millions of Honeywell's antipersonnel fragmentation bomblets ended up scattered over huge areas of Vietnam, Laos, and Cambodia. (An estimated 80,000,000 bomblets remain unexploded in Southeast Asia. Since the end of the war, over 60,000 civilians have been killed by accidentally detonating unexploded ordnance.)

Marv began by soliciting experienced leadership and participation from antiwar and community groups throughout the Twin Cities. The first official organizational meeting of the Honeywell Project drew about twenty-five people including Evan Stark, an antipoverty worker who would become a major player in the new organization, and Martha Roth, a Minneapolis writer and TCDIC volunteer who was a living example of goodness. The group quickly concluded that any effective attack on corporate weapons production would require a commitment of years, not weeks or months. They began to study the weapons, the corporate structure of Honeywell, the board of directors and their connections to other businesses, and the unions and workers at the weapons plants. They also brought in engineers, scientists, and economists to help develop peaceful products the company could produce without loss of profit or jobs.

I attended the first couple of meetings, but my plate was too full already. I was not able to commit to the workload participation demanded. I watched with great respect as Marv and his determined and uncompromising band pursued the war profiteers right here in our hometown. Then one night as I was leaving the TCDIC office late—I had been working on an article for an upcoming newsletter—I encountered Marv and two of his Project members leaving the Liberty House store. We chatted for a minute on the sidewalk, and I asked if they wanted to get a beer somewhere. The three of them exchanged some furtive glances, and then Marv leaned in and whispered to me, "We're going out to case one of Honeywell's munitions plants. Want to come along?"

How cool would that be, I thought to myself. We all piled into Marv's car and drove out to the plant. Some of the Project members had made contact with a few sympathetic plant workers who were willing to meet occasionally to share inside information, but one-on-one only, as they did not want to be identified with the Project and risk losing their jobs. These insiders had just revealed the existence of a large stash of bomblets with minor manufacturing defects, but no detonators, discarded in a hefty pile behind the plant. Marv wanted to get some of them to use as visual aids. Our task that night was to begin surveillance to determine if the guards patrolling the plant perimeter relied on a schedule.

The building itself was huge and surrounded by open space for equipment storage and large vehicle maneuvering, with a chain link fence eight feet high and topped with barbed wire. We only had to circle the complex once to spot the stash of bomblets in the back, about 200 feet in from the fence. The small service road we were on was probably used mainly for pick-up and delivery vehicles, and not a single car or truck came by the whole time we were there. We watched from midnight to 4:00 a.m. and duly discovered and noted the one patrol car with a flashing yellow light on top coming by precisely every thirty minutes, never slowing, stopping, or varying its routine in the slightest way.

One of our guys wanted to make a dash for the stash right then, but Marv wanted to scout the location at least one more night, and he also wanted to figure out a way through the fence rather than over it. It was not in the cards for me to join the mission again, but as I remember it, it was just a few more days before Marv had his antipersonnel fragmentation bomblets in hand. They were treacherous looking. They became menacing visual aids whenever Marv sat down in meetings with investors, the board of directors, or corporate executives, most of whom had never seen up close the dangerous devices they were profiting from.

The Honeywell Project continued to protest and to teach and inform the public about the company's military contracts well after the Vietnam War ended. In 1990 Honeywell spun off its munitions business, forming a new company, Alliant Techsystems, and claiming the pressure from Honeywell Project had nothing to do with their decision. Oh, really?

Marv Davidov spent his life working for peace and justice. He died on January 14, 2012, at age 81. Rest in Peace, Marv Davidov. Rest in Peace.

30

NIXON INAUGURATION

January 20, 1969
37,562 Dead

Peacemaker my ass. He wasn't called Tricky Dick for nothing, as we would all find out, though not soon enough. On this day he had the arrogance to claim, "The greatest honor history can bestow is the title of peacemaker." Excuse me, but in my opinion, you have not earned the honor of "peacemaker" if you continue a war that will claim the lives of another 20,724 of our young men. A true Peacemaker announces on this day, in this speech, the war in Vietnam is over. He had his opportunity for greatness, but he blew it.

He went on in his inaugural speech to say, "I shall consecrate my office, my energies, and all of the wisdom I can summon, to the cause of peace among nations." Instead he bombed the hell out of all of Southeast Asia. In the end his inauguration speech was nothing but platitudes, empty promises, and lies.

Nixon's campaign had emphasized his "law and order" issue and what the press dubbed his "secret plan" to end the war. The plan was labeled "secret" because Nixon remained vague on how he would bring about this "peace with honor." It is now known from the release of declassified information, including FBI wiretaps, that Nixon deliberately sabotaged Johnson's peace talks. He directed Anna Chennault, his liaison to the South Vietnamese government, to convince them they would get a better deal from Nixon if they refused the cease-fire being negotiated by Johnson and waited until Nixon won the election. The South Vietnamese chose to play ball with Nixon as President Thieu, a notorious gun and drug runner, refused to attend the Paris Peace talks, and the war dragged on. Nixon's illegal interference (see The Logan Act of 1799) was symptomatic of the lies he would tell throughout his presidency.

I am still confounded by how politicians can lie quite readily even though the lie costs innocent people their lives. There are apologists for both Nixon and Johnson who advise us to balance the mistakes of these men against their successes. I am not among them. The blood on their hands washes away any credit their other accomplishments ever earned them.

If only Nixon had held to the promise he made on November 7, 1962, at the Beverly Hilton Hotel. After conceding defeat in his race against Edmund "Pat" Brown for Governor of California, Nixon told the reporters gathered to cover his concession speech: "Just think how much you're going to be missing. You don't have Nixon to kick around anymore because, gentlemen, this is my last press conference."

31

Poets Resistance Tour

April 26, 1969
41,655 Dead

Rent and utilities for the TCDIC office; salaries (at the barest subsistence level) for full-time staff; paper, printing, and postage for our monthly newsletter to 1,500 subscribers; paper and printing for thousands of pieces of literature distributed to high schools, colleges, churches, and civic groups throughout the state every month—all these required an influx of cash that was not easy to maintain. We survived mainly on donations, including from some staunch supporters who made monthly pledges. We held art sales and yard sales, but money was always tight. We never did see (or seek) any of the Communist Party funding we were accused of receiving, so The Poets' Resistance Tour was a welcome shot in the arm for our bank balance.

Organized by the national arm of Resist to support local draft resistance groups in ten cities, thirty nationally known poets all waived their appearance fees, and most of them covered their own travel expenses as well. Each poet visited two or three of the cities on the tour. Minnesota Resist and TCDIC organized the Minneapolis events together, and Arnie Goldman, a University of Minnesota English instructor, took the lead role. So many advance tickets were sold, the poetry reading had to be moved from the campus Newman Center to the much larger Coffman Memorial Union Ballroom. An afternoon colloquium held at the Museum of Natural History Auditorium and moderated by Professor Chester Anderson focused the discussion on how political poetry could or should be.

I was particularly excited about the Dinner with the Poets event hosted by John and Ann Buttrick. I was taking and selling tickets at the door for those who wanted to enjoy a buffet dinner and meet and greet the poets before the reading. Tickets were ten dollars, which would be equivalent to over seventy dollars in today's money, making this an event primarily for faculty, and way out of the price range for most students or counterculture radicals.

A friend had recently pointed to a picture of one of our featured poets, Ed Sanders, on a Fugs album cover, and mentioned how much we looked alike. I had never been likened to anyone famous before, so I wanted to meet Ed in person to see how real the resemblance might be. He was ten years my senior, but judging by the album cover photo, we had the same shoulder-length, golden-brown locks parted from the same side and the same configuration of clean-shaved cheeks and chin with prominent mustache.

Not all of the poets were coming to the dinner, which made it a wait-and-see situation. I did not know if Sanders would even show up. Sitting at a card table just inside the front door provided me the perfect seat from which to see everyone who entered. And then they came: Robert Creeley and Ed Sanders together, arm-in-arm and laughing almost hysterically at some inside joke, each man carrying his own half empty (or half full) bottle of whiskey. Creeley had recently become (and still remains) one of my favorite poets, and Sanders was in one of my favorite bands. As they entered the room, they both stopped at my official looking little table with the sign saying, "Tickets $10," and Creeley fake fumbled in his pockets as if looking for money.

"I haven't got any cash," he said to me, and then he turned to Sanders and asked him, "Have you?"

Ed Sanders was staring into my eyes as if someone had said to him just before he came, "Hey, there's a kid there tonight who looks just like a younger you," and now he was staring into a mirror to his youth. I, too, was struck by our resemblance and would later tell my friend how right he had been, but at that moment I simply replied to Creeley's attempt at humor and said, "Gentlemen, you are the guests of honor, and dinner is being served." I gestured with my right arm toward the dining room and the laughing poets left. The dinner party was packed. I never did get a chance afterwards to chat with these poets because seekers of wisdom always surrounded them.

What especially impressed me about meeting these two men was the performance each one gave when it was his turn on the stage. I knew they had been drinking, how much I couldn't be certain, but when Creeley took the stage, he didn't miss a beat. His quiet tone with seemingly simple language and form expressed the depth of his insight with an uncommon clarity. Sanders appeared throughout the program between the other poets. He presented original songs and poems while accompanying himself on what he told us was not an autoharp although it looked like one. I forget what he said it was: a zither? A microlyre? He held our attention from start to finish, sometimes sitting cross-legged on the edge of the stage and other times reading from the lectern.

The local Twin Cities poets who graced the program included John Caddy, Keith Gunderson, Peter Weller, and Garrison Keillor. The nationally known poets who made the stop in Minneapolis were led by our own hometown heavyweight Robert Bly, who had won the National Book Award for Poetry the previous year for "The Light Around the Body," followed by Galway Kinnel, Carl Rakosi, Vern Rutsala, and Diane Wakoski. It was a literary extravaganza, and afterword we partied till dawn.

32

MILWAUKEE 14 TRIAL

May 14, 1969
42,581 Dead

Francine du Plexis Gray magnificently covered this trial and the movement the Milwaukee 14 represented in *The New York Review of Books*, an article well worth your effort to find and read (*The New York Review of Books*, Vol. 13, No. 5, September 25, 1969), so good, in fact, I will not rehash the whole trial here. My role was as a supporter of the Milwaukee 14 and an observer with a keen interest in how to approach the legal system when one has a political point of view one feels outweighs the importance of legal maneuvering.

I expected to go to trial myself before the year was out, and I was particularly interested in the Milwaukee 14's decision, just prior to the start of the trial, to release their attorney, the famed William Kunstler, and conduct their own defense. The federal prosecutors had decided to delay their proceedings until the state charges had been settled. They reasoned the defendants would have a more difficult time raising their political and moral arguments in state court against charges of arson, burglary, and theft. Boy, were they wrong about that. This group of antiwar activists probably had more advanced degrees between them than all of the rest of the people in the courtroom combined.

Soon after the "14" acted, Fred Ojile moved into the newly acquired Colfax House, where he would frequently hold discussion groups in his room. I remember one night when we were sitting around chatting and

Fred suddenly had one of those realizations that something wasn't quite right. "You know what," he said, "if you come up the stairway to the third-floor entrance, turn right down the hallway to my room, enter the room, and look to the right, the wall in my room is not all the way back to the entrance. There must be a secret room behind this wall."

Somebody got a tape measure right away. This was too intriguing not to investigate. Sure enough, there seemed to be an enclosed space six feet by eight feet behind the wall in Fred's room. There was not a full attic above the third-floor apartments, just a crawl space, so we had never thought of going up there, but there was a trap door in the hallway ceiling. Somebody got a ladder. In a matter of minutes, a half dozen of us were smoking a joint in our secret room. It was difficult to get in and out of there though, and I only remember one other time we used it. An AWOL soldier needed a hiding place for a night before he could leave for Canada, and that's where he slept. Although no federal agents or military police came looking for him, we felt he would have been safe in there if they had come.

Another member of the Milwaukee 14 who was a friend of mine was Doug Marvy. He was about six or seven years older than me, and I adopted him as a kind of big brother I could turn to for advice, which I did. Also because of his age, he was not subject to being drafted, so his respect for draft resisters who risked prison to take a stand against the war influenced his decision to join the Milwaukee 14 action.

The third member of the group who was from Minneapolis was Father Al Janicke. I did not know him well, but we had met at various rallies and antiwar meetings. I tried to attend as many as possible of the preliminary hearings and court appearances the group had to make so as to show the powers that be just how many people supported these men and what they had done. I would usually hitchhike to these events because it was the cheapest way to travel in the heyday of the Sixties. The three Minneapolis participants often left two or three days prior to an appearance in court in order to meet with their attorneys, but one time they left the day before, and Doug invited me to ride with him and Father Al, who was driving.

We were just twenty-six miles into the trip, still in Minnesota, when the good Father exited the freeway at Stillwater. "There is a little diner just down the road a piece with the best coffee in the world," he told us. "I have to have some." While it seemed a little silly to be stopping so soon, I didn't mind, as I was a bit hungry. We settled into a booth, the waitress came over, and Father Al said, "Coffees all around, please." I had been looking at a menu and was about to order some breakfast when the Father interrupted me. "No, no, no. We're just having coffee," and he shooed the waitress away. Then he leaned in to me and almost whispered, "There's a place just a half hour into Wisconsin that has the best breakfast in the world. You'll love it. And I have to have some." He was right, again. And again, and again as he had the best place for lunch, and later for pie, and then dinner, and finally cake. What should have been a five-and-a-half-hour drive took us twelve hours, but what a delicious twelve hours.

Two months before the Milwaukee 14 went on trial, I attended a benefit for the "14" staged by the Firehouse Theater in Minneapolis. Named for the old fire station they rehabbed and occupied on Minnehaha Avenue and Lake Street, this daring and innovative theater troupe was well known for their antiwar support. Director Sydney Walter, at thirty-one years of age already well past the top draft eligibility age of twenty-six, had publicly denounced the war and returned his draft card to his draft board. So, of course, they drafted him. With 200 people there, the demonstration in support of his induction refusal was the biggest sunrise ceremony I ever saw. The Firehouse Theater members put on a short antiwar play on the steps of the old federal building, and an actress from the company did a dance in the nude while she stabbed a melon with a large knife. I'm not sure what the symbolism was, but I enjoyed watching her act. Surprisingly, she was not arrested.

For the benefit, the Firehouse presented their original version of the Faust legend, which they titled, A Mass for Actors and Audience on the Passion and Birth of Dr. John Faust According to the Spirit of Our Times. When I arrived at the theater with several resistance friends, the lobby was already humming with anticipation, and there was a sizable crowd. I had heard nothing about the play in advance, so I harbored no expectations. This was a small theater, of course, and the entrance to the auditorium from the lobby was through two doors currently guarded by stone-faced actors with crossed arms. At the appointed time another member of the troupe advised us that the actors would escort us to our seats one by one and we should forget about sitting with the people we came with.

As I stepped up to the door, an actor/usher took my ticket and asked, "Do you want to be Faust or see Faust?" I had a hunch it might be more fun to be Faust, and that's what I replied. The actors must have known the floor plan blindfolded because it was much too dark to see anything. The actor seated me on the floor. When the lights came up, I found myself on stage with several other audience members. The rest of the audience sat on low benches radiating out from the stage. The actors were everywhere. Audience participation was encouraged, and I may have cried out or howled at some point. After two hours of intense drama, one of the actors announced the play was over. "However," he said, "we understand the play is quite complicated, so we are going to run through it again, from the beginning. If you wish to stay, you are welcome. If you wish to continue your evening elsewhere, we recommend the Black Forest Inn. They have excellent food and drink at reasonable prices."

At least half the audience then left the theater. He didn't fool me, though. I did not believe for a moment they would run through a two-hour play again. I stayed in anticipation of a surprise ending. Once again, the actors asked each one of us if we wanted to be Faust or see Faust. Surprisingly, some people still said they wanted to see Faust. They were escorted to the seats at the back of the room farthest from the stage. Those of us who still wanted to be Faust were all assembled on the stage. Then the actors draped a large parachute over the entire stage preventing the people who wanted to see Faust from seeing anything going on under our silk cloud.

Next the actors came out with basins of water and towels and asked each of us to remove our shoes and socks. Then they washed our feet. For the final scene the actors rolled out two tables laden with fruit, cheese, bread, and wine. People ate and drank and mingled and met and partied and then just drifted away. It was the crack of dawn when I finally left the best play I ever saw. But I digress.

Fast-forward to the actual trial. I approached for the first time the massive Bedford limestone Milwaukee County Courthouse from the east by crossing MacArthur Square, named for General Douglas MacArthur, who had attended high school in Milwaukee. One of the first of its many imposing details I noticed was that the three entrance doors bore the words "TRUTH," "JUSTICE," and "ORDER" chiseled into the stone façade above them. Was it coincidence "TRUTH" and "ORDER" were locked doors and "JUSTICE" was a revolving door? I thought not.

Not only was the courtroom packed, but the overflow crowd of supporters filled the hallway. I had by this time been in many courtrooms in support of other resisters and activists, and it had become commonplace for us to remain seated when the bailiff called out "All rise" preceding a judge's entrance, since we typically found little or no reason to show respect for jurists biased against us. So, of course, I remained seated for this judge's first entrance on the scene. A handful of seasoned activists scattered throughout the gallery remained seated with me, and the majority of spectators, most of whom were new to the world of trials, duly noted our attitude.

There can be quite a few breaks in these proceedings, resulting in a considerable amount of sitting and standing as the judge enters and leaves. At each successive break, more and more supporters joined the ranks of the seated. By the end of the day, Judge Charles Larson had had enough. He informed us we were showing disrespect to the court and the solemnity of the proceedings by not rising for him, and he would not tolerate it. Beginning first thing in the morning, anyone who did not rise for the judge when he entered the courtroom faced contempt of court charges and immediate arrest.

As we left the courthouse, I said to my friend Lynne, the beautiful, long-haired, guitar-playing artist I had met the night before at the rally for Milwaukee 14 supporters at the Highland Avenue Methodist Church, "Well, I guess I'm going to jail in the morning. Can I leave my backpack at your apartment until I get out?"

"Of course," she assured me.

We had time to grab a bite before heading over to the church for the nightly rally for trial supporters. There had to be close to 200 people there, way more than you could fit into the courtroom. There were two moderators who began the evening's discussion with the question of how we were going to respond to the judge's threat of jail. I could not believe all of the rationalizations I was hearing about why we should not go to jail. I understood many of the people in this room had never had to take a real stand by exposing himself or herself to risk or danger. They were proud of what the Milwaukee 14 had done but were not prepared to stand in those same shoes.

I was standing in place in the middle of the crowd to indicate I wished to speak and finally my turn came. I said something very close to this: "The men we are here to support are going to prison because they want to show the world how important and serious the cause they represent is. We would be doing exactly the same thing if we go to jail tomorrow. We should fill their jail to overflowing, and if they lock all of us up, we should fill those seats the next day and do the same thing. We should smother them with shame."

There were no risk takers who vowed to sit with me the next day in court. Instead, people again began to make excuses for why we should not go to jail. I understood. It is not a decision to be made lightly. I had already put in my time and careful introspection on this decision many months before this day, so I came prepared. But I could clearly see this group would not reach a consensus. I spoke to the assembly once more.

"We can debate this issue all night, but I will not change my mind. I will remain seated tomorrow just as I did today. I trust all of you to make your own decision for your own reasons." And then I left the meeting.

Lynne and I went back to her apartment where I began to analyze what the likely outcomes of my actions would be in the morning and how I might best prepare for them. I don't remember if I acquired this idea from someone else or if I came up with it myself, but I composed a note for the judge I would hand to one of the bailiffs before court started. It was short and simply stated: "My religious beliefs inform me the greatest respect I can show to anyone is to treat each person as my equal, so I am unable to show deference to you by rising when you enter the room, unless I do the same for everyone else who enters the room. Thank you for your understanding. Daniel Holland."

I really did not expect the judge to take this to heart. I merely wanted to have some, any, leg to stand on should I find it necessary to challenge on legal grounds a harsher sentence than anticipated. I expected a sentence of twenty-four hours for such an infraction, but you can never know for sure what is going to happen when you enter a court of law. Remember the front doors of this very building: "Truth" and "Order" remained locked and "Justice" was a revolving door.

First thing in the morning, I handed my note to one of the Milwaukee County Sheriffs serving as a bailiff and asked him to give it to the judge. He looked at me as if I was crazy.

"I'm just trying to avoid causing trouble," I told him. "You can read it first if you like." I had simply folded the note in half. It was not sealed. He took it and walked away. When the courtroom opened for spectators to enter, I tried to get as close to the front as possible so the judge would be sure to see me, but the number of spectators always far outnumbered the available seats, and I ended up in about the middle of the gallery on the aisle. Just before the proceedings began, the bailiff found me and leaned in to whisper in my ear, "The judge said you may remain seated."

I could not believe what I had just heard. The next voice I heard said, "This court is now in session. The Honorable Judge Charles Larson presiding. All rise." Because half of the spectators were in front of me, they did not see I remained seated. Most of the people behind me could not see me because the people around me were standing. Only a handful of people immediately near me were aware of my defiance. At the first break people asked me about my action, and I explained the judge and I had reached a special agreement, but I could not say if he would extend the same consideration to anyone else. Gradually a few individuals joined me in remaining seated, and nothing ever happened to us.

This trial was an amazing learning experience for me, perhaps it was straight out of the theater of the absurd. I would go on to use many of the tactics, arguments, and attitudes these brave men, the "14," had developed when it came time for my own trial.

Condemning the induction center as a threat to human life prior to my arrest on June 18, 1969. Photo by Heine, from the *Minneapolis Star-Tribune*. Courtesy of the Minnesota Historical Society.

33

BUSTED

June 18, 1969
44,115 Dead

We had a friendly source inside the U.S. Attorney's office who called the TCDIC office on June 13 the moment the grand jury issued its True Bill indictment charging me with "violation of Title 50, Appendix, United States Code, Section 462, to wit, . . . DANIEL A. HOLLAND unlawfully, willfully and knowingly did fail and neglect to perform a duty required of him under and in execution of the Military Selective Service Act of 1967 and the rules, regulations, and directions duly made pursuant thereto, in the defendant did fail and neglect to comply with an order of his local board to report for and submit to induction into the Armed Forces of the United States." I was, of course, in the TCDIC offices when the call came in, and before the clerk of court could finish swearing out the arrest warrant, I went underground.

The purpose of going underground was not at all to avoid arrest but rather to gain some time to plan how we might orchestrate the arrest under our terms instead of the government's terms. We wanted to use my arrest to bring attention to the antiwar movement. I fully expected Jim Redpath and a few of his U.S. Marshals to show up at the TCDIC office within the hour or to wait for me at Colfax House and nab me there, so I slipped away with Sandy Wilkinson and headed over to George Crocker's house. Nobody kept any minutes of the meetings that ensued, at least not any I have been able to locate all these years later, so I am not certain of everyone who participated in these planning sessions. My best guess is a core group of six to ten of us developed our plan and then invited those people we knew we could trust to keep it secret until the event occurred. We ended up with a group of 35-40 people.

One of the first ideas we discussed was to take sanctuary at the Quaker Friends Meeting House. George was a lifelong member of the Friends, but the year before he had taken sanctuary at the Universalist Church when the Friends Meeting had been unable to ratify a sanctuary motion. Now the Meeting had an open offer of sanctuary for any draft or military refuser. Any war. Ever.

George's sanctuary had lasted less than one day. Sanctuary does not enjoy any legal standing. The authorities are free to execute their arrest warrant inside the confines of any church, synagogue, mosque, or meeting house, and FBI agents had muscled their way through the crowd toward George. George, not wanting any violence to erupt, told his supporters, "We have made our point," and surrendered to the agents.

The main reason to take sanctuary was to raise public awareness of just how significant the resistance movement had become, and an arrest made in a public setting with a large group of supporters would be much more likely to receive press coverage than an arrest made quietly in someone's home. While sanctuary did afford the aura of spiritual approval, it seemed too much like passive resistance. I wanted something bolder.

One idea was for me to stay underground, not submit to arrest at all, to go on the lam, to leave the state altogether. As the idea of the prison doors closing on me became more real and more imminent, this idea had some appeal. But one of our main goals was to clog the federal court system with draft cases and we were approaching a fifty percent caseload in the District of Minnesota at the time. Besides, my plan all along had been to defend myself in court and present to a jury my own case against the war and the government. I wanted my day in court. I would not back down now.

I'm pretty sure it was Ed Plaster (yes, it had to be Ed Plaster) who came up with the idea we finally chose. Ed and I had been pushing the limits during our induction center leafleting sessions by going inside the building and talking with the men who were being inducted or taking physicals. The old federal building consisted of three floors of solid granite. The first floor had a large central lobby with a polished marble floor plus GSA and other miscellaneous federal agency offices off to the sides. The Armed Forces Examining and Entrance Station (AFEES), popularly known as the induction center, occupied the second and third floors. Ed and I had organized a handful of compatriots to join us in our forays into the interior recesses of the induction center.

One day Ed was manning the lobby, which offered the first chance to put a leaflet in the hands of an inductee. I was on the second floor with the other daredevils prowling the hallways and sneaking into the rooms where the inductees were being poked, prodded, and tested when I was startled by the image of Marine Sergeant Watashe coming up the stairs with Ed Plaster flung over his shoulder in a fireman's carry. As they reached the top step and turned down the North hallway, Ed nonchalantly waved to me from his position draped over the sergeant's back. I couldn't help laughing at this incongruous sight, but I was also concerned Ed must have been arrested and worried about what might happen to him in some back room. I quickly followed the pair to Captain Herring's office, where Sergeant Watashe dumped Ed on the carpeted floor.

There was no arrest. Sergeant Watashe had simply overreacted when Ed refused his order to cease leafleting inside the building. Now Captain Herring was trying to convince us we had to "go through the proper channels" to get permission to leaflet inside the building. When we argued that he allowed another group to pass out bibles on the second floor, he was unconvinced our informational flyers were comparable. Ed gallantly proceeded during the ensuing weeks to write a seemingly endless chain of letters "through the proper channels" to no avail, as each contact shifted the responsibility to yet another office. Meanwhile, we continued to press our disruptions inside the induction center as we tried to stop the flow of bodies into the war machine.

I guess because Ed was so immersed in these skirmishes inside the induction center the idea he suddenly blurted out in the middle of our brainstorming session seemed only natural: "Hey! Why don't you take sanctuary at the induction center?" Since we did not expect the concept of a safe haven to afford actual protection from arrest for me, why not create a safe haven for the men being inducted with me. We could condemn the building as a hazard to human life and invite the inductees to join us in resistance to war and a celebration of life. It was just crazy enough to work. It was certainly different enough to attract some press. Everybody quickly got on board. We wrote out a two-page flyer and printed it on our mimeograph machine. We chose Wednesday, June 18, as the day.

Organizing a demonstration like this required a considerable amount of grunt work, most of which I was spared, as I had to remain out of sight until the 18th. Keep in mind we did not have computers, email, cell phones, or social media. All telephones were tethered to the wall in those days, and no telephone could be trusted to be private. All contacts had to be made face-to-face. We only had a few cars we could use, so much of the contact involved hitchhiking and bus riding.

A demonstration of this nature was not lightly undertaken, so all of the participants, men and women, were dedicated activists who wanted to make a difference. They were duly informed they would likely face arrest for, at least, disrupting a federal office or disorderly conduct. Lawyers who supported the resistance movement would be standing by to represent everyone who was arrested, but no bail fund would be available. The risk of spending some time in jail was very real.

On the morning of the 18th, we gathered at the TCDIC office at 6:00 a.m. Doors to the old federal building opened at 6:30, and our plan was to enter the building at 6:45. We piled into our vehicles and drove over to the induction center, and then we drove around the block a few times to see if we could spot any sign the authorities had been tipped off. A couple of journalists had been alerted the night before, but they were trusted friends who we did not believe would call the heat and blow the story. The coast looked clear, so we made our move.

We expected the induction center staff to call the U.S. Marshal's office as soon as they spotted us. We didn't anticipate the demonstration would last even 30 minutes. The first members of our group attached large printed posters on the doors declaring the building "Condemned and unsafe for human life." The lobby was quiet as we entered. Someone brought the Flower Power banner reading, "War is not healthy for children and other living things," and hung it from a column. The Specter of Death was present in his long black robe and pasty white face, carrying his scythe for the reaping of souls while he read the names of Minnesota war dead. A few people stationed themselves near the doors to hand out invitations to join us to inductees. The rest of us gathered in a circle sitting shoulder to shoulder and linking arms in the center of the lobby floor. We sang protest songs as we passed around loaves of homemade bread and jugs of apple cider (we didn't want to complicate the expected charges against us with alcohol and contributing to the delinquency of minors as several of us were under twenty-one). Most of the young men reporting for induction took our two-page invitation/flyer, but none of them joined our circle. A few office workers from the building began to gather around the edges of the lobby to watch what was happening.

Everything was unfolding just as we had planned it. The U.S. Marshal's

Singing "We Shall Overcome" in the lobby of the induction center on June 18, 1969. Photo by Heine, from the *Minneapolis Star-Tribune*. Courtesy of the Minnesota Historical Society.

office was just four blocks away in the new federal building, so I was looking for Jim Redpath and a few of his men to enter the lobby at any moment, maybe scold us, and then arrest me. One of the journalists we had invited brought a photographer with him who had already taken several shots of our gathering. We had plenty of time to make the afternoon paper.

Then events took an unexpected turn. About a dozen cops from the Minneapolis Police Department entered the lobby, and Police Sergeant Ed Gunderson informed us our demonstration was unauthorized and ordered us to leave the building or be removed by force. We had the cops outnumbered three-to-one, but they had guns and nightsticks, and we were committed to nonviolence, which meant the outcome was a foregone conclusion. But we were not going to just get up and walk away. I approached the police sergeant and explained the U.S. Marshals would arrive any minute to arrest me and then the whole thing would be over with. He was definitely not satisfied with my explanation.

"You must leave the building immediately, or my men will remove you," he said.

"OK," was my reply, and I took my seat in the circle again. We all linked arms in order to slow the process of dragging us out. I still remember the casual, business-as-usual look in the eyes of the cop who sprayed mace in my eyes while his partner whacked me on the shoulders and back with his nightstick. Some of the officers grabbed people by the arms or legs and dragged them toward the doors. We were all trained in traditional non-violent protest tactics. We tried to hang on to each other as best we could without striking back at the police, but they broke us apart by clubbing our arms and legs. Then they dragged us into the street. The police removed all the protesters from the building except for the Specter of Death, whose photo appeared in the afternoon paper showing him standing alone in the lobby with his sign reading, "I win all wars."

Battered, bruised, and bloodied, eyes stinging from the mace, we scrambled into our vehicles and got the hell out of there. We were in no mood to wait for the U. S. Marshals to show up now. I grabbed the passenger seat in Sandy's car and yelled out the window to my friends, "We're heading for the Quaker Meeting House." I felt taking advantage of the Quaker's open invitation for sanctuary would at least give us some time to rethink our strategy.

At the Friends Meeting House, Ron, the administrator who handled the day-to-day operations of the community, met us. Friends do not have a minister or spiritual leader. Ron welcomed us and immediately saw several of our people were in need of first aid. He made one phone call to start a calling tree and then began to clean and bandage wounds. Within an hour, there must have been fifty Friends there. They were so kind and supportive we were quickly healed in spirit and our physical wounds seemed less troublesome. I may never be able to thank the Friends community enough for their efforts on our behalf.

We had just begun to discuss what options we might take at this point when Ron approached me, "You have a phone call in the office," he said. Most of the people I knew who might call me were in this building with me. As I walked with Ron back to his office, I was quite curious to know who was calling.

"Hello," I said into the receiver.

"Danny, I hope you and your friends are OK," replied the familiar voice of Jim Redpath. I knew Deputy Chief Marshal Redpath well because over the past year I spent many mornings at the induction center handing out leaflets and talking with young men ordered in for their pre-induction physicals or actual induction into the army. We were "allowed" to be on the sidewalk in front of the old federal building, but we were not "allowed" to hand out literature inside the building. But let me tell you, it gets pretty

Me (in plaid shirt) trying to negotiate with police seargent Ed Gunderson prior to thei police beating us and dragging us out of the induction center. Photo by Heine, from the *Minneapolis Star-Tribune*.

damn cold outside in the dead of a Minnesota winter. I would sometimes sneak inside the door to warm up on the most bitterly cold mornings. There were no building personnel stationed in the lobby of the building so if I huddled near the door, I could stay out of sight and still hand out my leaflets to people coming in. I soon learned if anyone who worked in the building did spot me, the standing orders were to call the U.S. Marshal's office to come over and remove me (or us; I often worked with a partner, and we took turns so no one person had to work the induction center every day). I also learned if I saw someone notice me, it would take about fifteen minutes for the marshals to get there from their office in the new federal building. I could continue to warm myself inside for ten minutes, and then wait outside for them.

The first time this happened, Redpath said, "Well, the people in the building said you were inside handing out your leaflets. You know you're not supposed to go inside, so I'm going to have to arrest you."

"You have got to be kidding me," I said, and I was incredulous because I knew that he knew the U.S. Attorney was not going to spend any time even considering prosecuting such a trivial federal charge.

"I'm not joking," he said with a straight face that fooled me the first time, and he took out his handcuffs and cuffed me. As we walked over to the Marshal's office, I told Jim how I knew he knew there would be no charges, so wasn't this whole exercise a bit silly. He kept up a good front all the way into the office, and then he took off the cuffs and offered me a cup of coffee and a chair. I accepted. Why not make friends with the U.S. Marshals, I thought. It might prove beneficial at some point down the road. Thus began our friendship. Over the next several months Jim must have arrested me close to a dozen times. It was our own little coffee klatsch. We would talk about the war and the draft and the protest movement. He was very sympathetic, but he felt the ballot box was the way to make change, even though I pointed out how the voting tactic wasn't working very well and too many people had died already.

Anyway, we liked each other, but now he had a very real warrant for my arrest, on a very serious charge, and he was on the other end of the telephone line.

"You heard what happened?" I asked.

"Well, you finally pissed 'em off with that one, Danny."

"So, what're you going to do now?" I asked him.

"I have a car with two Marshals parked in front of the Meeting House right now. Why don't you just walk out and turn yourself in so nobody else gets hurt?"

"I've got two reporters and a photographer in here with close to a hundred supporters. Why don't you come in and get me?'

"You know I can, but I don't want to risk injury to my men or your friends. You know you want to go to court. That's where your battle is. Let's just end this now."

"I'm staying put." I knew he was right, but I couldn't figure out a way for me to come out on top just yet.

"Listen," he said, "everybody's emotions are running pretty high right now. Let's just take some time to cool down and talk again in the morning. My men will be outside if you try to leave, though."

"Fine," I said.

We had no central leadership within the resistance, of course, but the full-time staff generally acted as a central committee of sorts. I engaged that resource for help in deciding how to proceed, and together we decided there were basically two options: turn myself in or maintain the sanctuary. I was still stinging from the beating we had taken, physically and emotionally, so I wasn't ready to give in yet. We went into the main meeting room to present our options to the assembled supporters, now numbering about

Nonviolent resistance: tug of war between police and protester on June 18, 1969. Photo by Heine, from the *Minneapolis Star-Tribune*. Courtesy of the Minnesota Historical Society.

forty people from the resistance community and at least fifty people from the Friends community. I explained to people that I felt like staying in the sanctuary as long as the Marshals were going to stay outside, but I couldn't do it without their support. I wanted to hear from everybody. There was no right or wrong position to take. It was most important to be honest about the level of commitment you were willing to make.

Then a woman from the Friends community stood up and spoke. I don't remember her name, but she had beautiful long gray hair and was eloquent in her voice and her presence. She invited all of us to participate in a meeting for worship. The Society of Friends, she explained, holds a central belief all people are endowed with a measure of the divine spirit. Worship is a gathering in reverent silence, filled with the desire to draw nearer to God and one another. The Friends do not, she went on, have one person designated as the minister, and all in attendance share equally in the service in ministering to one another. Those who feel led may speak out. Those who keep silence and those guided to speak yield their minds and hearts to the guidance of the spirit.

This was an invitation I was honored to accept. It was a new experience for my resistance supporters and me. We sat in silence for at least an hour interrupted only a few times by brief statements from community elders. George spoke once, too, but he had a lifetime of experience in meetings. This service washed away my anguish.

Dinner was our next agenda item. The Friends community started bringing in food, and we feasted. Political talk resumed with the meal. If I was going to stay in sanctuary, my draft counseling schedule hours had to be filled by other counselors. Committees I was on would have to meet here, or without me. The Free University course on resistance I was co-teaching with Scott Alarik would have to meet here, or without me. And the same applied for another course I was co-teaching with Harold Henderson. My first day of sanctuary was spent rearranging schedules, and I was suddenly struck by how much time I would be left just sitting there.

The day passed into night and most of the Friends left, although there was an overnight contingent staying with us. Then Ron asked for attention and explained there would be a few rules requested by the members of the Friends community. First, a request we refrain from coarse language, and we were fine with that. Please, no smoking on the property. Although many of us were smokers, we could respect the rule. And girls would sleep on this side of the room and guys would sleep on the other side of the room–he gestured to the right and the left. You could hear a sigh from the assembled young lovers accustomed to cuddling at night, but no one raised an objection. We were guests of loving, caring, peaceful people in their house of worship, and we did not want to create an unhappy experience for them.

At this point in my life I was not in an intimate relationship myself, but I had great sympathy for those supporters of mine who were. By morning I began to feel I was asking too much of the people who were there for me: to protect me with their bodies when they had already taken a beating for me; to take over my responsibilities for counseling, committees and teaching when they had busy schedules of their own, and were putting their love lives on hold by sleeping on the floor in segregated quarters. I realized we had chosen the induction center "sanctuary" over the traditional sanctuary in a religious building because we had wanted to create an event for publicity. We got our publicity with an article and pictures in the paper. We were in sanctuary now simply because the arrest itself had not happened as anticipated, but we had achieved all of our other goals. What was the point now of disrupting all of our lives over a waiting game with the feds? After consulting with the core, I decided to turn myself in.

I still had conditions to negotiate, though. I called Jim Redpath and said I would like to find a way to end our standoff.

"What have you got in mind?" he asked.

"Well," I said, "I can't just walk out to the car where your men are. They will have to leave. And I can't just walk into your office and say, 'Here I am.' You'll have to send your men over to our office to pick me up."

"Danny, how do I know you won't just disappear?"

"Come on, Jim. You know I want my day in court. Besides, we're friends. I wouldn't treat you that way."

"What about the press, Danny? I don't want the press."

"I'll make a trade with you. I'll send the press home. I'll tell 'em it's over with. You promise not to cuff me when you take me in. I don't like handcuffs."

"Deal. What time?"

"Give me a couple of hours."

"Don't go past 3:00 p.m. I want enough time to process you or you'll have to stay overnight in the lock-up."

"Got it. Thanks, Jim."

"Yeah. Bye."

We had a deal, and I was confident we would both live up to it. The reporters had already gone back to their offices; I called them and told them the confrontation was off. Then we watched for our federal friends parked in front to leave. Once the coast was clear we went back to our office where I called Jim. I just wanted to get the arrest phase over with now.

Jim arrived with two of his deputies and we made it out to his car and drove downtown without incident. They did have to fingerprint and photograph me first, and then they brought me in front of Judge Devitt for a bail hearing.

Devitt asked if I had an attorney. I told him I would be representing myself.

"I'll let Judge Lord worry about your lawyer. He'll be your trial Judge. Bail is set at $2,000 cash." (the same as $14,154.00 today.) All of the draft resisters publicly involved in the movement who were arrested before me had received personal recognizance bonds, so this was a bit of a shock. There was an audible gasp in the courtroom. There is no way I would be able to raise that kind of money. My immediate reaction was, "Well, I start serving my sentence today." I wasn't quite ready for lock up yet, but I knew I'd better get ready fast. Devitt told his clerk to move on to the next case on the docket, and one of the marshals escorted me out of the courtroom. Jim Redpath was right behind us.

"Danny, this has got to be a mistake," he said to me. "Wait here. I'm going to try and talk with the judge."

"I'm not going anywhere," I said, as if I could have just gotten up and walked out. Nobody even cracked a smile.

It was over an hour before Redpath came back. "The Judge agreed to your personal recognizance bond. They just have to sign some papers in the back, and you can go."

"You are the best marshal in the business," I said with a sigh of relief. I will always remember the kindness and friendship of one Jim Redpath.

34

ARRAIGNMENT

July 23, 1969
45,126 Dead

Back to basics. I liked draft counseling. I felt I was making a difference in at least one man's life. Immediately. Many times I helped restore a lost deferment when induction was imminent, so I immersed myself in my counseling duties while awaiting arraignment.

I received a notice in the mail from the clerk of court to appear in Judge Miles Lord's courtroom for arraignment on July 23rd. I had made up my mind I would defend myself in court, but I anticipated resistance (no pun intended) from whichever judge drew the case. I sought the advice of the attorneys who had become vigorous supporters of the draft resistance movement: Chester Bruvold, Ken Tilsen, Larry Leventhal, and Jack Graham. They all warned me none of the federal judges for the District of Minnesota would welcome a defendant who chose to defend himself. They were in agreement that all of these judges would do their best to prevent such a scenario from occurring in their courtroom.

I felt these excellent lawyers had already made the technical legal arguments and constitutional challenges against the Selective Service System in the cases of Dave Gutknecht, George Crocker, and others. Any repetition of these assertions in my case would be redundant. Noncooperation was our response to the Selective Service System, and it seemed to me now was the appropriate time to use noncooperation as our counter to the legal system as well. Why should I hire a lawyer? I refused induction on moral grounds. Our country's history was full of examples of immoral laws, from slavery to Jim Crow, and I wanted to make my case before a jury of my peers in my own words, from my own mouth.

If I could persuade the jury the war was immoral and convince them they could help bring it to an end by voting not guilty, together we could make headlines and put every potential juror in draft cases on notice that they had the power to decide the most important issue of the day. Or, if I could convince just one member of the jury to vote not guilty, resulting in a hung jury and a mistrial, I would still generate local headlines and spark the discussion before juries to come.

Then I got a call from Jack Graham. Judge Lord had contacted Jack and appointed him to represent me in court. Apparently Judge Devitt had alerted Judge Lord about my plan to employ a self-defense strategy for my trial. Hoping to thwart the possibility, Judge Lord had summoned Jack Graham to his chambers and appointed him to defend me. As an officer of the court, Jack could not refuse the appointment even though he was well aware I intended to defend myself, but he did want to give me a heads-up he would be in court on the 23rd.

I arrived early enough to meet with Jack in the hallway before we went into the courtroom and explained that my plan for this arraignment was to object to everything Jack said in court in order to rattle Lord's cage. Jack understood but reminded me he was under orders from the Judge to make a legal record on my behalf. We understood each other.

The courtroom had a single long table shared by the defense and the prosecution, not the two separate tables we usually see on TV dramas and in the movies. Jack and I took our place at one end of the table and Assistant U.S. Attorney Ralph Koenig came over to us and shook hands with Jack but completely ignored me. His attitude annoyed me, but I had no desire to establish any rapport with the man who was trying to send me to prison. I ignored him as well.

The bailiff called the court to order and announced my case as the first on the docket. The judge welcomed everyone and then addressed me directly.

"Daniel Holland, I see you are represented by counsel."

"No, I will be defending myself."

"As I am sure you know, I have appointed John Graham to represent you, which is why he is sitting at the table with you now."

"Yes, you have appointed him, but I have not hired him, nor do I recognize him as my attorney."

"Danny, I am sure you have heard the saying a lawyer who defends himself has a fool for a client. I don't want to see you do anything foolish. Mr. Graham is here to make sure you have the best possible defense. You should take advantage of his expertise."

"Miles, I am not a lawyer or a client, so I am not worried about playing the fool in these proceedings. And Mr. Graham has not been appointed to protect my interests, he has been appointed to protect your interests. We all understand that."

"Danny, the proper form of address when speaking to a judge in a Federal courtroom is to say, 'Your Honor,' or 'Judge Lord,' or 'Judge.' The court considers it disrespectful to use first names."

"Miles, the greatest respect I can pay any man is to treat him as my equal. If you are going to use my first name, especially the familiar form, then it is only respectful I do likewise with you."

"Well, I can hardly call you 'Your Honor' or 'Judge.' How about if I call you Mr. Holland? Would you be willing to call me Mr. Lord?"

"Oh, you can call me 'Your Honor' or 'Judge,' either way is fine by me. But if you prefer to go with 'Mister,' I can live with that."

"Good. I'm glad we got that settled, Danny."

"Me too, Miles."

The humor of our exchange seemed to go right over his head. We would see each other in court every month for the next nine months, and he would always revert to calling me "Danny," and he would always be upset when I responded with "Miles." I would have to remind him of our agreement to use "Mister" when speaking to each other, but I swear he could not make it through a hearing without falling back on the familiar. He never addressed the attorneys, the bailiffs, the jurors, or the witnesses by their first names, only me. For now, though, we would just proceed with today's arraignment.

"How do you plead," the Judge asked me.

"I'm not making a plea," I answered, "until Mr. Graham has been dismissed."

"Mr. Graham, will you enter a plea on behalf of your client."

"Yes, I enter a plea of not guilty, Your Honor."

"I object!" I jumped in.

"You can't object to your own attorney," the Judge scolded me.

"I do not recognize him as my attorney. You and Mr. Koenig and Mr. Graham are all being paid by the government and have the government's interests at heart, not mine. I still object."

Scott Sandvfick and Scott Alarik, playing guitar respectively in center and at right, lead the assembled in song as a dozen young men sign a letter refusing to register for the draft at the Universalist Church on March 5, 1969. Photo by Krueger, from the *Minneapolist Star-Tribune*. Courtesy of the Minnesota Historical Society.

"Your objection is noted. That concludes the proceedings for today. The clerk will notify you when to appear for preliminary hearings." And Judge Lord hurried out of the courtroom.

"Well," I said, turning to Jack, "that didn't go too badly."

"We're off to a flying start," Jack said, and we both laughed.

I went for coffee with a few friends and then headed home. I had not put myself on the counseling schedule or planned any meetings because you can never be sure how long you're going to be in court on any given day, or whether you'll even remain free by the end of any court appearance. At home I would be able to work on various writing assignments without the inevitable interruptions bound to occur in the office.

When I walked into Colfax house, Scott was in the living room with a young woman I had never seen before. Petite, light brown hair, blue-eyed; she radiated beauty.

"Danny," Scott said, "This is Mary Berg. She's considering moving into Colfax House in the fall. She came to your arraignment this morning and wanted to meet you."

I took Mary's hand in mine, to shake it, and sparks started to fly, although no one else noticed it. I tried to pretend I was calm, and everything was normal. I offered to do the tour for her, and together Scott and I showed Mary all three floors of our big house, ending with my room at the back of the house on the second floor. We sat on the edge of my bed looking out at a pair of mourning doves cooing in the blue spruce just outside the window and sharing our coming-of age stories, even though we were all still very young.

Then Mary opened the notebook she had been carrying with her and said, "I made a drawing of you in court today." She handed me an exquisite pencil sketch done on the lined notebook paper. It portrayed a monstrous ogre's hairy face with evil eyes and threatening fangs, with spittle shooting from an engorged tongue. The ogre's face had no body, but it did have talons protruding from the bottom of its head. Held tightly in the grasp of these talons was the cutest furry little creature with one little teardrop falling from its left eye. (I cherished her drawing even though it was just a pencil sketch on notebook paper. I put it in a frame and had it in my room for several years until one night during a party it disappeared.)

As the afternoon wore on, we started to tire, we all leaned back on the bed, the pauses in the stories grew longer, and just as I sensed I was drifting off to sleep, I felt Mary's hand touch mine and our fingers intertwined. I awoke with a start when Mary suddenly sat up and exclaimed, "What time is it?"

I glanced over my shoulder at my bedside clock. "4:20," I said.

"I have to leave," she said.

"Can I see you tomorrow?" I asked.

"I leave for Europe with my family in the morning. I'll see you when I get back and move in here." Then she kissed me on the cheek and left. The sparks stopped flying off me, but they continued running up and down my spine and across my skin, raising goose bumps on my arms and the back of my neck.

"How am I going to get through the summer waiting for her to come back?" I asked Scott. He had just moved into Colfax House in June, taking over the third-floor turret room vacated by Rick Sklader, who had left at least a hundred copies of Mao's Little Red Book behind. At just eighteen years old, Scott was already possessed of a deep intellect. He could more than hold his own in discussions of current events, romantic poets, contemporary fiction, or almost any topic that might come up, especially folk music. He was also an accomplished guitar player who could mesmerize with his golden baritone. Scott had led a group of sixteen high school students who publicly declared their refusal to register for the draft, and

Me with Mary Berg at Colfax House in October 1969. Photo by Gordon Raup.

continued his work as a high school organizer, helping to found the student unions across the Twin Cities that would fight for student rights as well as support antiwar and anti-draft rallies.

"It's not like you'll have time for pining away," he told me. "We're too busy for such silliness, and I'm here for you, buddy." And he certainly was. We spent many nights walking around (and I do mean literally all the way around) Lakes Harriet and Calhoun and sometimes Lake of the Isles, engaged in deep talks about love and life and pinball. We liked to watch the sunrise, too. The summer flew by. Then Mary moved in at the end of August.

Sparks did fly between us. It was not just my imagination. We quickly became almost inseparable. Both of us had our work responsibilities, but otherwise we were together. By the end of September, Mary moved into my room. The first thing she did was set up an easel at the foot of the bed. Starting with a blank canvas and working from the center out she gradually created an organic image in shades of gray, first with long strokes of thin paint then building up thick sculptural slabs. She worked the painting for a couple of hours and then stepped back from the easel. This was my first full look at the canvas, and I said without hesitation it was stunning.

The very next night when I came home, Mary was on the foot of the bed attacking my favorite painting with orange paint, I mean really going at it. "Oh. My God! What are you doing? Your painting was beautiful as is."

"Yes," she said, "but it wasn't finished." And she went back to work. Over the next several days she would add blue, green, red, yellow, but she instructed me not to freak out each time I came in the room and witnessed change happening. I learned to trust her judgment. Finally, she completed the painting. Its abstract flow of color and shape resonated with energy and emotion. I had to admit this final stage was better than it was at any single step along the way.

But there's more. One day Mary came home excited about an opportunity to participate in an invitational exhibition. The only problem, she told me, was she had just the one painting to offer. Then she had an idea. Before sharing her idea, she wanted a promise from me I would accept her artistic decision and support her in whatever decision she made. I assured her I had learned my lesson well. So, she said, she wanted to cut the large painting up and make several small paintings out of it. I pretended to remain calm. I probably said something like, "Oh, cool." I helped her cut the large canvas up into five new paintings and frame those smaller sections. She sold three of the paintings at the exhibition.

Even though the phrase "Think outside the box" had not yet become current, I had just been schooled.

35

THE AIRPORT INCIDENT

September 10, 1969
46,548 Dead

One night, Dave Gutknecht invited me to attend the New Mobe meeting (New Mobilization Committee to End the War in Vietnam), a coalition of all the different antiwar groups in the Twin Cities co-chaired by Dave and Bill Tilton. We shared resources among the groups in order to enhance individual projects and also planned major events together. We were making plans for the upcoming National Moratorium Against the War in October and the march on Washington in November.

A few of the smaller groups asked for volunteers to help with ongoing projects. A fledgling chapter of Vietnam Veterans Against the War particularly attracted my attention. This group was distributing a newspaper called *Vietnam GI* published out of Chicago by and for servicemen. The local VVAW was seeking volunteers to help staff the airport and bus terminals. When a draftee finished basic training, he was generally allowed a short leave home before shipping out to Vietnam. After their leaves, these soldiers would take commercial flights from their home cities across the country to the West Coast, where they would board ships bound for war. As it happened, many of these soldiers would have to change flights in Minneapolis. Volunteers were needed to make sure someone was always at the airport to hand out papers to soldiers waiting for their next flight.

While I thoroughly enjoyed the major events we helped to organize, I especially appreciated the opportunity to engage one on one about the war, the resistance, and the direction of our country. I volunteered for four hours one night a week at the airport handing out free papers to soldiers. Perhaps it was my small-town naiveté, but I truly believed we could change the world one person at a time, thereby growing our movement with each heart and soul we inspired.

Airports were very different in 1969 from what they are today. The only security check was at the approach to the jetway, and passengers and their families and friends were free to wander around the terminals as they wished. I just strolled the airport checking the waiting area at each gate for soldiers and wandering into the bars and fast food nooks.

It also happened that at the time airports had become overrun with Moonies, Hare Krishnas, and other religious groups accosting travelers and trying to sell them books, photos, incense, or just get a donation from them. Everyone who flew was annoyed by this obnoxious invasion of space.

Then the federal government passed a law prohibiting solicitation at airports. I was not selling the VVAW paper, though. It was free to service personnel, five cents for civilians, and I was only looking for soldiers. I would not have sold a paper to a civilian even if they asked me because just one such sale would most likely result in me getting kicked out of the airport. Some nights I met as many as a dozen soldiers, other nights I met only two or three. Not one soldier ever refused the paper. Whatever their stand on the war, they wanted to read it.

One night I saw a young soldier sitting by himself. I walked over and sat next to him, introduced myself, and asked if he would like a copy of a newspaper published by soldiers for soldiers.

"It's free for people in uniform," I said.

"Yeah, I'd like to take a look at it," he replied.

I told him how I was just a volunteer passing out the papers, and I had never been in the military myself. I told him how I had joined the draft resistance to oppose the war and my trial was coming up soon. He told me where he was from, but I do not remember that detail (we knew each other for such a very short time). He said he was being shipped to Vietnam to fight for our freedom. That's what they told him in basic training he said, and he had no reason to doubt it. He was very young. He might have been 18 or 19 at the most. I was all of 20.

Just then an airport police officer approached us and said to me, "Did you just sell this soldier a newspaper?"

"No way," I said. "I gave it to him. It's free for soldiers, five cents for civilians. But I wouldn't sell one to a civilian even if they asked me, because that's not allowed in the airport."

"Well, you still can't pass out free papers," he said. "You better come with me."

"Look," I said, "I'm not doing anything wrong. We're just talking. And I'm not going anywhere unless you arrest me." I really didn't think he would arrest me because doing so would have been ridiculous. And ridiculous it was.

"Okay," he said, "you're under arrest. We'll let my captain sort this out."

"Wait!" the soldier jumped in. "Don't arrest him. Here, I'll give the paper back," and he tried to hand me the paper.

"No! No!" I said leaning back and pulling both my hands away from the paper. "Didn't you just tell me you're fighting for our freedom? Don't let this guy take away your freedom to read a newspaper."

"You're coming with me," the cop said.

I stood up. The soldier stood up. I held out my hand and he shook it.

"Don't worry about me," I said. "I know lots of lawyers. I'll get out of this easy. You take care of yourself."

I harbored no concern for myself, as I understood this officer's overreaction to the situation would not even reach the courts because the police would simply look foolish for pursuing it. But I was concerned about my young friend. He was heading to war, and the dangers he faced were far more real than mine. But maybe, just maybe, this would be the incident that caused him to rethink his support of the war. As the officer led me away, I looked over my shoulder and saw a look of dismay on the young soldier's face.

The arresting officer, dressed in police blues and wearing a holstered pistol, was now leading me through an area of the airport most people never see, the police department offices and lock-up. Sitting behind a large desk was an officer wearing the same blue trousers but a white shirt with important looking insignia and no gun.

"Chief," my officer said, "I caught this guy passing out papers in the airport." The Chief leaned back in his chair, put both of his hands behind his head, and looked me up and down.

"Now I know you know you're not supposed to do that," he said.

"I know you're not supposed to SELL papers," I told him, "and I'm not. I'm just giving them free to the handful of soldiers who might be in the airport tonight."

"Let me see one those papers," the Chief said.

"Well," I said, "they're free for servicemen but five cents for civilians."

"Give the man a nickel, Bob," the chief told my arresting officer. Bob didn't like that, you could tell by the look on his face, but he dug in his pocket and pulled out a nickel. I put it in my pocket and handed the Chief a paper. He looked it over for a couple of minutes, reading some headlines and picture captions I suppose, and then he said, "The law is pretty clear. There are no solicitations of any kind at the airport. I think we're going to have to write you a ticket."

"It would be my pleasure to see you in court on this one," I said. "It will be a slam dunk in favor of freedom of the press. The top civil liberty lawyers in the state are already on board. Write me the ticket."

"Hold on there, Mr. Lefty. I don't even know who you are yet. How about you show me some ID?" I handed over my driver's license. The Chief examined it for a moment and said, "Okay, Bob, escort Mr. Holland to the visitor's lounge while I run a check on his identification."

The visitor's lounge was, of course, a six by eight-foot cell with a metal bench for sitting or sleeping and deadbolt locks deep into the floor, the ceiling, and the wall. An elephant could not have busted out of there. There were no windows, just concrete and steel. I sat on the bare metal bench and contemplated my situation. The chief would be checking my ID for warrants, which he wouldn't find, but he would probably see I was under indictment for refusing induction. I thought he seemed smart enough to figure out I wasn't kidding about going to court over a rinky-dink ticket and what a huge waste of his time such a losing battle would be, but I also figured he would want to back up officer Bob for hauling me in, which meant the punishment phase of these proceedings would begin right now. I resigned myself to spending the night in this lock-up, and I curled up on my bench, no pillow or blanket, figuring the time would pass faster if I were asleep. It was pushing 10:00 p.m. as I dozed off. Right around midnight came my wake-up call. It was officer Bob.

"Alright, you're free to go. But don't be passing out papers in the airport anymore."

"Yeah, right," I said, slipping into the night.

36

THE EDGE OF THE WORLD

October 10, 1969
47,197 Dead

Women's issues were becoming an increasingly significant topic in movement circles, and TCDIC was not immune to the discussion. Certainly the draft resistance movement was male dominated in part because only males were drafted. But most of us were also raised in a culture that supported and promoted the male leadership role. As women all around us began to challenge restrictions on the place of women in politics, education, business, the arts, and even in the antiwar movement itself, men in the movement had to confront their own prejudices and chauvinism.

I think having consensus-based decision making in our organization, without having a top-down hierarchy, made it easier for women to have their voices heard and for men to hear them. I don't mean to imply it was always smooth sailing. Men didn't always want to confront the issues women deemed important, and women were bringing those issues not just into the office but also into the home, the personal relationship, and even the bedroom. Some men were able to adapt and contribute to the conversation while other men were not.

When Leah Rutchick and Judy Hiemel approached me about the position of "head" or "lead" draft counselor, I took their concerns seriously. Sandy Wilkinson was the lead counselor when I joined TCDIC, and he trained me. He also set up seminars with our movement lawyers—Ken Tilsen, Chester Bruvold, Larry Leventhal, and Jack Graham—who taught us a great deal about the technical mistakes we could look for in a client's Selective Service file. Lead counselor basically meant the most experienced counselor and the one responsible for training and scheduling. We had to have a trained counselor in the office during all office hours, and the lead counselor had to fill all the hours when no one else was available.

When Sandy left TCDIC to become a counselor at the American Friends Service Committee, I became lead counselor by default, because I had the most experience and had demonstrated ability. Now two of our full-time counselors, Leah and Judy, were telling me the head counselor position ought to be filled by a woman. All of the male draft counselors were draft resisters and likely to be in prison within a year, they reasoned. I was probably at the head of the prison list, they pointed out. Why wait for a crisis moment to make the transition? I agreed with Leah and Judy that there was no point in waiting to transfer the post. They made their case at the next weekly staff meeting, and Leah took over as lead counselor.

This freed time for me to work on new things, and I decided to tackle our speakers' bureau. Up to this point, the speakers' bureau was basically an inbox for mail. Any written request for an antiwar or draft resistance speaker went into the inbox, and all of us read through the requests and selected the ones we were willing and able to accept. If a group called on the phone seeking a speaker, their information was written down and placed in the inbox. Now I would take on the role of coordinator, thus saving everybody time and hassle. I would assign speakers on a rotating basis, taking into account speaker preferences for large or small groups, specific topics or areas of expertise, and dates available.

We would send a speaker to any group, class, or organization at no charge, but we did ask people to give the speaker an honorarium if they could. Speakers could keep any speaking fees, which were quite welcome additions to our subsistence salaries. One day I opened a letter from tiny Assumption College in Richardton, North Dakota, from a young faculty member who was looking for an antiwar speaker who could also spend a day doing draft counseling, as they had no such resources available. He said the school could pay for round-trip airfare and an honorarium of $80.00. Well, that would double my salary for the month! As the new coordinator of the speaker's bureau, I assigned myself the job.

If you look at a map of North Dakota, you will see Richardton is a long way away from anywhere and 500 miles from Minneapolis. The airplane (on my first-ever flight) took me to Bismarck, where the faculty guy (let's call him Phil, I'm sorry I can't remember his name) and two students met me. We then drove 75 miles west before arriving at the college. I swear there was nothing to see along the way. I mean nothing. Phil gave me a tour of the campus culminating in the cafeteria, which had a huge glass wall looking out on the northern prairie. The dormant October landscape was colorless as it merged with the solid gray sky at the horizon.

"We're not at the edge of the world here," Phil said to me as he pointed into the distance, "but you can see it right over there."

I laughed appropriately at his joke, but as I strained my eyes to peer into the distance, I was pretty sure I could see the edge of the world. I wasn't in Minneapolis anymore.

My student hosts then took me to my accommodations for the night, a big old Victorian house that stood at the peak of a slight rise in the terrain, possibly the closest thing to a hill in all of North Dakota. Used for guest speakers and lecturers, the house had three bedrooms, a fully equipped kitchen, living room, dining room, and study, but I was the only one staying there that night.

I needed a few items I'd forgotten to pack, so the students took me into town to the local grocery emporium. As I was selecting a toothbrush, I heard hushed voices in the next aisle over.

"We're going to that draft dodger's speech tonight at the college, and we're going to teach him a lesson. You in?"

"Oh, I'm in. Should I bring anything?"

"Yeah, your baseball bat."

"Got it."

I heard their footsteps fade as they walked away, but I didn't want to walk to the end of the aisle and begin the confrontation right away. Where were my students? I needed some backup. Just then the students came around the corner, looking anxious. They had been two aisles over and had overheard the same conversation.

"We should call the police," one of them said.

"No," I said. "Think about it. Whose side are the police most likely to be on? Besides, it's just talk at this point. Can you get me a baseball bat, though?"

I didn't think my detractors would be foolish enough to attack me at the speech or even in front of any witnesses. My concern was they might wait until after the speech and try to break in to the guesthouse while I was sleeping. I wanted the baseball bat just to make it a fair fight. Although concerned about being outnumbered, I wasn't going to ask these students whom I'd just met to get into the middle of a fight for me.

The rest of my afternoon was booked solid with counseling sessions, which kept my mind off the incipient threat. At my speech in the evening, it seemed like the whole student body was present, maybe a hundred or more students, and about 25 to 30 townies. I used my "History of Vietnam" speech, because most people simply didn't know the Vietnamese people had a three-thousand-year history of defeating invaders by never giving up. You could actually watch people realize this war was never going to end unless we left.

I would always end with a question and answer session, and by this point in talks college audiences were generally pretty much against the war, although you usually had at least a couple of gung-ho war supporters who relied on emotion rather than logic or facts to express their undying, unquestioning loyalty to the government. Tonight that role belonged to the townies. A middle-aged man in the back of the room stood up and called out in a loud voice, "If you hate America so much, why don't you go to Canada with all them other draft dodgers? It ain't far from here, and we'll give you a ride right now."

"First of all," I replied, "I don't hate America at all. In fact, I love this country so much I am willing to go to prison trying to correct the mistakes our government is making. Second of all, you are breaking the law right now by offering to take me to Canada. The Selective Service law specifically forbids anyone from advising, aiding, or abetting any man to avoid the draft by leaving the country, or refusing induction. This is the law Dr. Benjamin Spock and several others are being prosecuted for right now. And you, sir, just might be the next one. I must warn you the FBI does follow me wherever I go (I was making this up), as I am not allowed to leave the country while out on bail awaiting my trial. There may well be an FBI agent or two in this audience tonight. You are the one breaking the law right now, not me, and you are the one most likely to be arrested."

The student body gave me a hearty round of applause for my response. The townie turned around and left the building, shadowed by a half dozen of his own followers. I accepted I would not change every heart I encountered along my path, but I did hope my FBI comments would deter these detractors from any ideas they still harbored about teaching me a lesson with their baseball bats.

When the Q and A period ended, my student hosts and several of their friends escorted me back to the guesthouse carrying enough baseball bats to fend off any band of rednecks we might encounter and enough beer to quench our thirst afterward. The baseball bats went unused in the end, and

some hours later the beer was gone. I had a full day of counseling scheduled the next day, beginning at 8:00 a.m., and I needed to get some shut-
eye. At first my protectors wanted to stay the whole night, but I convinced
them the hour was late and our antagonists had surely returned to their
homes and families by now. I slept fitfully, cuddling my baseball bat.

The morning came too soon, and I was at work before I knew I was
awake. Coffee gets the credit for carrying me through a day of nonstop
counseling until 4:00 p.m., when my hosts told me we had to leave for the
airport. Most of the students I had counseled that day had relatively minor
problems that were easily addressed, but two of them had more serious
difficulties and I would need to see their files before I could help them. I
advised both of them on how to go to their draft boards and make hand
copies of everything in their files (draft boards did not allow photocopies
to be made) and send them to me. I would figure out a course of action, or
their best options, and advise them by phone. I had spent the day in a re-
served classroom with a window facing south and sunshine streaming in,
but we cut through the cafeteria with its wall of glass on our way out, and I
was able to catch one last glimpse of the edge of the world.

37

My Trial

November 3, 1969
47,642 Dead

This really should have been a play. I wish I had had the foresight to secure a transcript of this puppy. But as much as I believed the work we were doing was important, I was not looking at it in terms of something I might want to write about someday. I was living in the moment. We were all living in the moment. Besides, I would not have had the financial wherewithal to afford the transcript.

Then one Friday morning I was sitting in the back of Judge Lord's courtroom in support of a friend who was being arraigned when the Judge spotted me and called me out by name.

"Danny Holland. I see you sitting in the back."

"Yes, Miles Lord. I see you sitting up there in the front," I replied, maintaining my strategy of always using the same format for names he used when addressing me.

"I have been thinking about your trial, and I may have come up with a solution for us. I propose we permit Jack Graham to sit at the defense table with you. That way you can ask him any questions at all you might have during the trial, but you will be able to conduct your own defense as you see fit."

"As long as I am in charge of my own defense, and you won't require Jack to make opening or closing arguments or any motions on my behalf, I won't mind if he's just sitting there. He's a good friend."

"Good. Good. What do you say we get started on Monday?"

"That works for me."

"I'll see you on Monday, Danny. Right here. 9:00 a.m."

"I'll be here, Miles."

It had been three months since my arraignment. Four courtroom appearances and three private meetings in Lord's office had left us in a stalemate regarding my right to defend myself at trial, which I would not give up and he would not give in to, and now we had finally reached a compromise during an unscheduled, informal courtroom chat. While I tried to maintain a respectful adversary demeanor in court, Lord had a tendency to speak patronizingly, not only to me but to attorneys and jurors as well. When we met in the privacy of his chambers, from which he would dismiss even his court reporter, and it was just the two of us, he became a better listener and spoke to me in a fatherly tone rather than condescendingly. I think when we were alone like that he was able to eschew the performer role he seemed to enjoy playing in the courtroom.

We still didn't make any visible progress during these private meetings, in part, I suppose, because I never wanted to say out loud, on or off the record, that I was guilty of this crime. For one thing, I did not consider my actions to be a crime. I considered refusing induction to be a moral duty and even a legal responsibility. Judge Lord did not want the jury exposed to these ideas because he was bound by the narrow confines of the judicial system, which asked only one question: Did the defendant commit the act (e.g., rob the bank, kidnap the person, refuse a lawful order for induction)? The defendant's reasons for committing the act were considered immaterial and inadmissible.

I'm sure the judge also wanted a competent attorney representing me because a number of draft cases, even in Judge Lord's courtroom, came down in favor of the defendant due to legal irregularities executed by poorly trained draft boards. Lord didn't want any reversals of a verdict from his courtroom being handed down by the appeals court on the grounds a defendant was not adequately represented by counsel. Any such technical defenses that might be available to me had already been argued in court in other cases and were currently being appealed to higher courts. They could only be redundantly argued in my case. And, as previously stated, I wanted to make my moral case to a jury of my peers.

The first order of business on Monday morning was jury selection. The bailiffs escorted a panel of 30 prospective jurors into the courtroom, and the judge interviewed them for general bias and potential conflict of interest. The judge excluded two of them from the panel. Then the prosecution and the defense were to alternate with peremptory challenges until twelve jurors and two alternate jurors remained. I declined to strike anyone from the list and asked the prospective jurors, "Who am I to judge any of you? Can I look at you," and I pointed to a woman in the front row, "and say you are not fair? Can I look at any of you," and I pointed directly at a man in the back row, "and say you are fair? No. I will trust each of you to obey your conscience today and do what you know is right."

This tactic meant the prosecution made all of the jury selections, which might appear to stack the jury against me, but these were exactly the people I needed to reach with my message, and my message included the idea that each of them possessed a conscience, and they would need to listen to it. At lunch my friends and supporters were anxious to share with me their belief that one of the jurors just might be on our side. He was the youngest one at age thirty and had a big, droopy mustache and longish hair. I reminded my friends we were not the people who judged others by their appearance. I believed if the prosecutor had felt there was any chance Mr. Mustache would cause a hung jury, he would not have been sitting there.

The defense presented first. In my opening statement, I told the jury how the prosecutor and the judge would both be telling them their consciences didn't matter. They were to decide this case on a narrow point of law. Nobody, I assured them, not even the judge, could decide for them that their consciences did not matter. Their consciences would tell them what was right. All I wanted to do was to share with them what really went on in Vietnam and what the protest movement was all about. To do this, I explained, I would call as witnesses a Vietnam combat veteran and several draft resisters who would speak about the reasons to oppose the war and stop the killing.

I then called my first witness, Gordon Neilson. Gordie wore his army uniform to court and cut an impressive figure at six feet tall, with broad shoulders, dark hair, and medals on his chest. He put his hand on the Bible and swore to tell the truth. Then before I could ask my first question, Assistant United States Attorney Ralph Koenig addressed the judge.

"Your Honor, I object to this witness on the grounds of his relevance to this case."

"Very well," the judge replied. "I will hear this testimony outside the hearing of the jury, and then decide on its relevance. Bailiff, escort the jury to the jury room." After the jurors were safely out of hearing range, I proceeded.

I asked Gordie, "What was it like in Vietnam?" You would have to have a hard heart indeed not to have a tear in your eye after listening to Gordie Neilson tell about the death and destruction he witnessed and committed. It would not be proper for me to try to reconstruct Gordie's story from memory all these years later, but I can assure you it placed a heavy emotional burden on those who were there to hear it. Sadly, none of the testimony in this trial was preserved in the National Archives. Judge Lord then made his ruling.

"While the testimony by Mr. Neilson was emotional and dramatic, it does not aid the jury in determining a fact in issue. The prosecution's objection is sustained. The jury will not hear Mr. Neilson's testimony. Mr. Neilson, you are excused."

Next I called Alexander Wilkinson to the witness stand. Sandy was my friend and mentor, and I simply wanted him to tell his personal story of how he came to feel compelled to commit civil disobedience to oppose the war. The same procedure used to exclude Gordie's testimony was followed: objection, removal of jury, testimony given to judge, objection sustained, witness excused.

Guess what happened when I called Donald Olson and Scott Alarik, who were also friends and allies in resistance? You guessed it. As my final witness, I called myself to testify. There was no objection from the prosecution. I told the jury I wasn't going to play some game where I asked myself a question and gave myself an answer. I just wanted to talk with them for a few minutes about what we were all doing here on this day. I summarized the testimony of the witnesses the court denied them the right to hear and suggested this testimony was kept from them because it may well have influenced the jurors to render a verdict unsatisfactory to the government.

Then it was the prosecution's turn to present its case. Koenig opened by telling the jurors exactly what I told them he would say. Their job was to decide a single fact: did Mr. Holland refuse a lawful order for induction or did he not? The war in Vietnam was not relevant. Mr. Holland's conscience was not relevant. Their consciences were not relevant. We lived in a nation of laws so we could live in an orderly society. People could not go around picking and choosing which laws they would obey and which ones they would not. Only chaos could follow from such choices. When we disagreed with laws, we had the ballot box to make changes. Mr. Holland may be sincere, but he broke the law, and he knows he must pay the price for doing so.

The first witness against me was a woman from Caledonia who was the secretary for my local draft board. Under questioning from Koenig, she established she did receive a letter from me containing my draft card and my statement refusing to cooperate with the Selective Service System. She testified I made a personal appearance before the draft board and reiterated my refusal to cooperate after which the board reclassified me 1-A Delinquent and issued an order for me to report for induction on September 23, 1968. She and I knew each other, because everyone from a town the size of Caledonia knows each other. She knew I was a good kid from a good family, but I'm sure it was difficult for her to understand why I had become this radical antiwar protester. I did not cross-examine her. She stated the facts accurately, and I had no desire to put her through the wringer for doing so.

I did not understand why the prosecution called their next witness. I have chosen not to name him here because I am going to accuse him of lying under oath, and the man is now dead and unable to defend himself. (If it is important to you to know his name, you will be able to find it if you dig deep enough, which seems to me like a lot of work for a little payoff.) This witness was a Navy commander and was the highest ranking officer stationed at the Minneapolis induction center at the time. He testified that on September 23, 1968, after I had refused to step forward and take the oath to enter the military, his lieutenant escorted me to the commander's office where I presented him with a two-page statement with my reasons for refusing induction. He read the statement completely, pleaded with me to change my mind, and then asked me to sign the statement, which I did.

It was all a lie. The lieutenant had taken me to his own office, explained the commander was not there that day, offered me the chance to change my mind, asked me to sign the statement, which I did, and then wished me good luck. Why didn't the prosecution call the lieutenant to testify since he was the actual witness? Did they think the higher-ranking commander would be a more impressive witness for the jury than the lieutenant? Was it worth the risk to tell this lie in what should have been a slam-dunk case for the prosecution anyway? Was the commander lying because he was not supposed to be away from his post on that day and he was protecting himself? I could not answer any of these questions, but I felt outraged by the deception.

Of course, I decided to cross-examine this witness. The trouble was I had never seen any episodes of "Law and Order," as that show had not yet been created, so I had no idea how to cross-examine a hostile witness who was lying. I did have Jack Graham sitting at the table with me, and I could have turned to him for advice, but then I would have proved Judge Lord right, and I couldn't countenance such an idea. I was stumbling along in my questioning of the commander, trying to trip him up Perry Mason style, probably confusing everyone in the courtroom about where I was going with this line of questioning, when Judge Lord interrupted me saying, "But Danny, you don't deny that you refused induction, do you?"

"Miles, really, you can't ask the defendant that question from the bench."

"Oh, you're right, as a point of law, I cannot ask you that question. The jury will disregard my question to the defendant." Having won this point, I decided to cut my losses and ended my questioning of the commander.

"You are excused," I said to him. He left the witness stand with a smug look on his face. He was the only other person in the courtroom who knew that he lied, and he knew he just got away with it. He knew I knew, though, and there was some small satisfaction for me in that.

The prosecution rested its case. All that remained now was to make our closing arguments and hear the jury instructions from the judge.

I presented my closing arguments first. I told the jury that they had all heard "My country, right or wrong," but that phrase was only part of the statement given by Senator Carl Schurz of Wisconsin on the Senate floor on February 29, 1872. What he said in full was, "My country, right or wrong; if right, to be kept right; and if wrong, to be set right." I said that it was incumbent upon all of us in the courtroom to set this country right again and end the war. I went on, Mr. Koenig told you in his opening remarks he knows I am sincere in my beliefs, but I know I must pay the price for breaking the law. Yes, I am willing to pay the price, which is why I am here instead of in Canada. People who oppose the war and flee to Canada are demonstrating their own self-interest. People who stay here and fight the draft in the courts and in the streets are demonstrating their true patriotism. The country's leaders have made a terrible mistake, and thousands of Americans have lost their lives for it. You can make a statement to the whole nation today by saying we will no longer send young men to prison for refusing to fight this war.

I continued, saying that after World War II the victorious allies held war crimes trials in Nuremberg, and many of the defendants in those trials tried to absolve themselves of any responsibility for the Holocaust by saying they were just following orders. The Nuremberg Trials, Principle IV, now states, as a foundation of international law, "The fact that a person acted pursuant to order of his Government or of a superior does not relieve him from responsibility under international law, provided a moral choice was in fact possible to him." This is my moral choice, I told the jury. This is your moral choice.

I reminded the jury once more that the prosecutor and the judge would be telling them they could not rely on their consciences to make their decisions. I also reminded them they would have to live with the decisions they made. I thanked them for their service and for their patience with me, and then I invited them to join me at the TCDIC offices for coffee and cake. However they voted today, my friends and I would welcome the opportunity for conversation.

Koenig kept his closing arguments very brief. He could have skipped them altogether, because I had already told the jury exactly what he was going to say. He told them their consciences and morals were not at issue, their political views were not permitted, and the law required them to decide a simple issue of fact.

Judge Lord then read his instructions to the jury. Fourteen instructions in all, most of them boilerplate rules for a jury to follow in almost any federal criminal case, but I will quote in full the fourteenth and final instruction from the judge, the last words the jury would hear before they began their deliberations:

"I again instruct you that you have a very limited responsibility in this case. It is solely to make a determination under these standards which I have enunciated to you whether this man is guilty or not guilty; that's all. You have no philosophical or religious or theological responsibility at all. Counsel has made some observations to you which might occasion in your mind the thought that you have some responsibility to determine the wisdom or the lack of wisdom in this government's policy in Vietnam or foreign affairs generally; that might question the wisdom of Congress in enacting the Selective Service Act; that go to the very basis of the right of an individual to have his own independent thoughts in this country of ours.

"Well, I advise you that you have no such responsibility. If the war in Vietnam is wrong, if the selective service is wrong or if other things are wrong in this country, the remedy lies in the political arena, it lies in the halls of Congress or in the executive branch of government. In our own tripartite system of government in this great representative republic, the responsibility for government is vital; the responsibility of Congress to enact the laws, even bad laws if they have a mind to, bad in the minds of many; the responsibility of the executive to enforce those laws; the responsibility of the judicial branch to interpret them, to apply them to particular fact situations.

"Here we are now in the whole scheme of that government applying our responsibility to the limited job we have in the judicial branch of the government. You jurors are a branch of the judicial branch of the government when you are called from your homes and offices to sit as triers of fact under our judicial system of jury trial.

"You said, each of you, when you were chosen as jurors, that you could be and that you would be fair and impartial jurors. I asked you if you would sitting as jurors find the facts to be as they were presented in court and if you would interpret the law as the court gave it to you, and each of you said that you would, and that is your sole and limited responsibility in this case.

"I have no doubt that this young man is very sincere and very honorable in expressing his beliefs, but as I say to you, we are not sitting here as judges of those beliefs, whether they are right or wrong, whether the government is right or wrong for legislation, policies for the conduct of foreign affairs. Your sole responsibility is to determine whether or not the government has proved beyond a reasonable doubt the allegations that are contained in this indictment. You said you would be fair and impartial jurors, and the court has every confidence that you will be fair and impartial jurors."

The judge then ordered, "that the jurors be kept together under the custody of officers until they have agreed upon a verdict or have been discharged by order of the court and that the marshal furnish such officers and jurors with all necessary meals and lodging during said period." It was 4:54 p.m.

No one, not even me, expected a lengthy deliberation. Most of my friends and supporters joined me in the courthouse cafeteria for coffee, and I had not even finished my first cup when a bailiff approached and informed us the jury had reached a verdict. We all returned to the courtroom, and when they brought the jury in it was exactly 5:30 p.m.

The jury took thirty-six minutes to decide not just the fate of one young man, but to decide to forego any responsibility for the lives of the soldiers being killed every day and the fate of the nation as a whole. I had thought they might take at least an hour to argue the point, but I was wrong.

I had hoped for at least one person on the jury to see the light, to hold out for a not guilty verdict, but I knew that was a lot to ask. I did not feel disappointed or let down by the verdict. My resolve remained firm. My friends and I went back to the TCDIC offices and brewed up a huge pot of coffee and ate cake. None of the invited jurors showed up.

38

D.C. MORATORIUM

November 15, 1969
47,931 Dead

Being free on bail pending appeal of my conviction meant I was not allowed to leave the state of Minnesota without permission of the court. Everybody in the country already knew the November Moratorium against the war was going to be the biggest demonstration ever held in the nation's capital, but there was no way I was going to ask Judge Lord for "permission" to attend. I was going. I didn't think the FBI would really have time to keep an eye on me with hundreds of thousands of people making their way across the country. So what if I got caught and Judge Lord revoked my bail? I would earn credit for time served toward my eventual sentence and get out of prison that much sooner. I would call that a wash.

The New Mobilization Committee to End the War in Vietnam was a coalition of antiwar groups taking the lead in organizing this event as it had taken the lead in organizing the previous October's hugely successful moratorium. In towns and cities across the nation, students, working men and women, the young and the old, people from all walks of life, met in churches, schools, and street rallies to voice their opposition to the war. Upwards of two million protesters participated in the events of the day. Minneapolis was no exception. Over 10,000 people gathered in front of Coffman Memorial Union on the U of M campus for speeches and then marched down Washington Avenue to the Old Federal Building on 3rd Avenue South where the induction center was located. After more speeches, singing, and chanting, as the rally began to disperse, a renegade group of about 200 protesters broke away from the main crowd and spilled onto Nicollet Mall, off the approved route for the march. A cadre of police officers carrying riot sticks quickly formed and started moving toward the protesters. It looked like there was going to be a fight.

Then Bill Tilton showed up. Bill was a member of TCDIC staff but also the Vice President of the Minnesota Student Association and one of the lead organizers with the New Mobe. He did not want to see an otherwise peaceful and successful demonstration by 10,000 people devolve to a fight between the police and a minuscule number of protesters. He went up and down Nicollet Mall pleading with the agitators to break it up, leave downtown. "You're not doing any good for peace this way. We've served our purpose downtown," he cajoled them, and one by one or in groups of three and four he single-handedly convinced these people to leave before violence broke out. Years later, Bill would tell me that was the proudest moment of his career. (I can certify his was and is an illustrious career.)

We were preparing to march on the nation's capital in numbers far exceeding any demonstration that had ever been staged there. Thursday evening, November 13th, was the beginning of the event in Minneapolis with a mass rally at the National Guard Armory where several young men turned in their draft cards or announced their refusal to register. Immediately following the rally, a number of buses left for Washington with those of us who wanted to participate in the March Against Death, which began at 6:00 p.m. Thursday and would continue through Saturday morning. This march would include almost 50,000 individuals—a number from each state equal to the number of U.S. war deaths from that state, plus a number representing destroyed Vietnamese villages—and would form a solemn procession starting at the Arlington National Cemetery and marching single file past the White House and on to the Capitol. When a marcher reached the White House, he or she was to stop, face the building, and call out the name of an American serviceman killed in Vietnam or the name of a Vietnamese village printed on a placard the marcher was carrying and then proceed to the Capitol where the marcher would place the placard in one of the caskets that would then be presented to the White House on Saturday along with the demands of the Mobilization. The draft cards and nonregistration statements from the Minneapolis rally would also be deposited in the caskets. The Minnesota contingent in the March Against Death was scheduled to march from 8:00 p.m. to midnight on Friday, so we hit the road on Thursday night.

I don't remember how many charter buses were hired to make the trip, but I do remember I didn't have the money to ride in a nice, comfy charter bus. Mary and I had planned to hitchhike, until a couple of brothers who supported the resistance decided to buy an old school bus literally the day before we had to leave and called TCDIC to offer as many seats as we could fill at no charge. I wish I could remember their names, but I have not been able to find anyone who does. They were great guys, though. Both of them knew how to handle the big bus and shared the driving, just the two of them, all the way there and back, over 1,100 miles each way.

The engine compartment was next to the driver's seat and opened up right inside the bus if you needed to do some engine work. They had crafted what appeared to be a brake fluid reservoir, but it had just a tiny amount of brake fluid visible when you opened the cap. If you left the cap on and detached the reservoir's two anchoring bolts, you could flip it over and expose the perfect hiding place for marijuana in the false bottom of the reservoir. Later on, that hiding place would prove useful.

We drove all night. On Friday, maybe around midday, we were cruising through the Blue Ridge Mountains of Pennsylvania, nearing the Maryland border, and somebody noticed a highway patrol car had been following us closely for quite a while. We all started watching him through the back window, making sure he knew we were watching him, and sure enough another highway patrol car came up behind the first one. The brother who wasn't driving came down the aisle to collect any pot people had and put it in the hiding place. We didn't know for sure what excuse they were going to use to pull us over, but we were quite certain they would ask to search the bus. If we refused, which would have been within our rights, our trip could be delayed considerably. We all agreed we should let them search because we had such confidence in the hiding place.

Before long there was a third car, unmarked, with four guys wearing suits in it, and we knew they were the guys who would want to search us. Then the two patrol cars put their emergency lights on, one stayed behind and one pulled alongside, and over to the shoulder we went. The brother who was driving was appointed the spokesperson and would do all of our talking. The four guys in suits came to the door and the uniformed officers each took up a position, one at the back of the bus and one at the front, with their hands on their still holstered pistols. The suit cops wanted to see the registration, of course, and explained that in Pennsylvania if you bought a school bus for personal use, you had to paint it some other color than orange. A school bus full of longhaired peaceniks had obviously been converted to personal use. Our driver explained this was not the rule in Minnesota. Since he registered the bus in Minnesota, he explained, it was legal.

"You might be right," the suit cop agreed, "but we ran the plates, and it's registered in Minnesota as a school bus. What is it doing in Pennsylvania?"

Our man explained how he and his brother just bought the bus on Wednesday, spent Thursday morning filing the registration paperwork with the DMV, and left Minneapolis Thursday night. The DMV had the paperwork, but they must not have finished processing it. (Keep in mind the DMV did not have computers at the service windows in those days. Finding this record would have meant convincing somebody over the telephone to figure out where this paperwork was on its route to a data-entry desk.) The suit cop invited the bus driver to sit in the cop car with him while they tried to verify the registration with Minnesota.

"In the meantime, you don't mind if we search the bus, do you?"

"Go ahead. We're not so dumb we would bring something illegal on a cross country trip to a major protest in a school bus."

The three other suit cops boarded the bus and instructed all of us to exit the bus, stand outside at the rear of the bus, and stay off the highway. With the patrol cars at the front and back of the bus still flashing their emergency lights and the twenty-five of us lined up behind the bus, all of the passengers in every passing vehicle could plainly see we were under siege, and at least every other car honked the horn. Many of these people were certainly on their way to the same protest march and flashed us peace signs—two fingers in a V raised high. The two uniformed patrol officers were watching over us with their hands still on their holstered weapons. I can't even imagine what they thought we might have done, but there was nothing for us to do except wave back at our fellow travelers as they passed by on the highway.

The second brother/owner of the bus had stationed himself outside the door of the bus while the suit cops searched. They started at the back of the bus and worked toward the front. When they got up to the driver's seat and engine compartment, they called the brother in and asked him to pop the hood on the engine, which he quickly did. They checked it over and even opened the lid on the fake brake fluid reservoir, but they didn't find a thing.

With the search completed the suit cops came over by all of us and started chatting it up while we all waited for the first cop and our driver to finish tracking down the registration. I was just hoping they wouldn't start running ID checks because they might find out I was not supposed to be outside of Minnesota. I guess they figured it would take too much time to run an ID check on everyone. Finally, the first cop and our driver came back with the good news—everything checked out and we were free to go. The whole stop took about an hour and a half. We were thrilled to be on the road again, but we waited until we crossed the border into Maryland before we fired up a couple of J's.

It was dark already when we arrived in D. C., but we still had a couple of hours before the Minnesota contingent was scheduled to begin its phase of the March Against Death. We arrived at our designated staging area for buses from Minnesota, and our driver brothers explained the bus would stay in this one spot until we left at midnight Saturday. At least one of the brothers would remain with the bus at all times, and we could leave our packs there if we wanted to. They emphasized the bus would leave promptly at midnight on Saturday. If you were not there when the bus left, you were responsible for finding your own way home.

Mary and I then made our way to the Metropolitan AME Church, which was our reception area to join the March Against Death. Shuttles were ferrying people to Arlington National Cemetery, where the march started. When we arrived at Arlington, organizers gathered us into groups to give us our instructions for the march. We were informed a shortened route was implemented because the government decided it would be too disruptive to continue to the   Capitol after passing the White House. The new route ended right at the White House, where the caskets would receive our placards with the names of deceased soldiers. We were also asked to remain silent for the duration of the march, as it was intended to be a solemn affair. The March would probably take at least two hours to cover the two and a half miles. As we exited the Cemetery, we would pass tables manned by volunteers who would provide us with a placard with a name on it. If we personally knew someone killed in Vietnam, we could request that name on our placard, or they could give us a name from the list of the 47,931 war dead. Upon our arrival at the White House, a volunteer would direct us, one by one, to approach the casket, turn and face the White House, call out the name on our placard, and place it in the coffin.

When we got to the placard table, I requested the name of BILL QUIL-LIN. Less than a week before we left for D. C., my mother had called to tell me Bill had been killed in Vietnam. She didn't have very much information, just that he was riding in a helicopter when it crashed. There were no survivors. Bill was in the class right behind me at Caledonia Public High School. We played football together. He might not have been the best player on the team, but he was big. We put him in the center of our defensive line, and the opponents couldn't move him. He was our run stuffer. He was also a kidder. He liked to goof around and to make his teammates laugh, even if it was at his own expense. He was good at that.

As Mary and I made our silent way along the march route and across the Potomac River, I tried to picture Bill Quillin as a soldier in Vietnam. I couldn't do it. He didn't have the killer instinct. I wondered how I could have missed him when he reported for induction because I was at the induction center at least two or three times a week passing out leaflets and talking to guys about their alternatives. More than once I helped somebody get out of an induction order. I blamed myself for not being there every single day. If only I had been there the day Bill came through, I might have been able to help him at least delay his induction. If he had not entered the army on that day, then he wouldn't have been on that helicopter on November 5, 1969, and he wouldn't be dead today.

The silence of the marchers had the intended effect of making the procession solemn. As we neared the front of the line, we could see now why the line moved so slowly. Each person who arrived at the front of the line was told to take the last fifteen paces alone, stop in front of the casket, and in his or her loudest voice call out the name on their placard before placing it in the casket. The rest of the miles-long line stopped and waited for each marcher's moment of truth.

When I approached the front of the line myself, I had an image of Bill strapped in his helicopter seat, rifle slung over his shoulder, and I thought I could hear the chop-a-ta, chop-a-ta, chop-a-ta of the helicopter's rotor. I don't know. Maybe there was an actual helicopter hovering above the march. I was filled with sadness. I was filled with rage. At the casket I turned and faced the White House.

"BILL QUILLIN," I screamed at Richard Nixon, who was known to be in the White House at that moment. Other marchers had been loud when they called out their names, but I was piercing. I wanted Richard Nixon to know he was responsible for this death. Nixon would later comment to reporters that he was watching some college football games when the March Against Death had come by his residence, and he had not really paid any attention to it. But I know his blood had to run cold at the moment I screamed.

The marchers dispersed in all directions after the casket ceremony, and Mary and I went in search of food, although we remained in silence. The emotional impact of this event was numbing, and I was close to tears. I didn't want Mary to see me cry. Even though I knew she would understand and accept me and love me as much as ever, I wanted at least to appear strong.

Saturday dawned at a chilly 30 degrees, which was no big deal for our Minnesota contingent. Filled with marches, speeches, sing-a-longs, and teach-ins, the day ushered in a feeling of community and lifted me out of the sadness of the previous night. The half-million people attending the protest were truly representative of the nation's diversity—young people, old people, students, workers, black, white, Latino, Asian—all coming together to tell our government what we expected of it. Our voices were loud, and we would be heard.

At dusk, Mary and I decided to go to the Department of Injustice, because Abbie Hoffman and Jerry Rubin were planning a demonstration there. Although the New Mobe did not sanction it, we just wanted to see what these creative tricksters might come up with. We edged our way through a crowd of 50,000 gathered at the building until we got to the front of the throng, where we faced a line of police in riot gear standing should-to-shoulder. As we arrived, the police commander used a megaphone to address the crowd, telling us we had one minute to disperse, or they'd fire tear gas at us. I don't think even five seconds ticked off before the first tear gas canisters came down at the front line of the protesters. Mary and I turned to run. Then the police started to lob tear gas canisters over the crowd so there was nowhere to run except into the gas. Then the canisters started to land in the middle of the crowd. One of them struck me in the back and the combination of that blow plus the heavy concentration of tear gas engulfing me brought me to my knees. Mary somehow found me in the chaos and tried to help me up.

"Run . . . run," were the only words I could get out. I thought I would just lie there in the street and let the police pick me up. Mary wouldn't have it, though. She put my arm around her shoulders and got me onto my feet, and somehow, we made it out of there. What a brave young woman.

There were still protesters everywhere, but the numbers thinned out because people had run in all directions away from the Department of Injustice. A few people were coming towards us, and a middle-aged woman came up to us and looked in our eyes, holding our faces in both of her hands.

"You need first aid," she said, pointing up the street. "At the first corner up there, turn right. In two blocks you'll come to a first aid station."

We staggered the few blocks to the aid station and were quickly treated with a solution of baking soda and water, which seemed to help a bit, but the stinging in the eyes lasted a couple more days and, in the lungs, even longer. The best medicine was just finding people who cared enough to help us.

We managed to make it back to the bus before midnight, but our clothing was saturated with the tear gas, and we couldn't get on the bus without gassing everyone else. Our friends formed a circle around us, with their backs to us, enabling us to change discretely into the one set of extra clothes we had each brought on the trip. Then we stuffed our tear-gassed duds into my duffel bag and tied it to the outside of the back door on the bus. Our clothes made it all the way back to Minneapolis, but we never found a way to get the tear gas out of them, and never wore them again.

39

MY SENTENCING

January 12, 1970
48,973 Dead

Early one morning shortly after our return from Washington, I was reading the newspaper in the TCDIC offices while waiting for the first pot of coffee to brew, when Martha Roth came in. Martha was one of the many dedicated volunteers who staffed our phone lines, scheduled counseling sessions, collated literature, greeted walk-ins, and managed the myriad of office tasks necessary to keep our organization humming. There were dozens of people who put in volunteer hours every week. On this particular morning, Martha casually mentioned she and her husband Marty and their three kids would be going to Mexico for three months. Marty had a one-trimester sabbatical from his teaching position with the U of M English Department, and they were looking for someone to house sit for them while they were gone. Did I know anyone who would be interested, she wondered.

As a matter of fact, I offered, Mary and I had been contemplating moving out of Colfax house so we could have some private time together before prison split us apart. Martha liked the idea of having friends she knew take care of the house. We agreed that I would call her in the evening after Mary and I talked it over. Mary dug the idea as well. We called the Roths and committed ourselves to the deal.

Their house was a cozy bungalow with a master bedroom on the first floor and two kid's rooms upstairs, plus a combination teacher's office, writer's study, and library. It came with a huge and very old Siamese cat and a pair of gerbils we were charged with keeping alive. And it came with a car, their beat-up old VW bug, the classic Sixties car. I loved their library because Marty had many books he taught in literature courses, with his notes in the margins. It was like auditing his courses. I remember he opened up Mailer's *The Deer Park* for me, which I had been unable to unlock for myself because, even with the worldliness gained through the resistance, I was still encumbered with the small-town youthful naiveté some people say I still possess to this day.

I still believe house-sitting the Roth's place was the right choice for Mary and me. We got to have dinner together, just the two of us. We got to have breakfast together, just the two of us. We got to play house. It was our opportunity to experience what life would be like together, and even though this would result in our parting ways, I still believe it was easier for us to do on our own than it would have been in the community atmosphere of Colfax House.

My sentencing was quickly approaching, and the thought of it loomed large in our decision-making process. Although I knew intellectually Miles Lord was going to give me time in prison, I was always optimistic that my moral courage would eventually sway someone, if not the jury, then maybe the judge. Until the gavel came down, there was a chance Judge Lord would join me in a public protest against the war and proclaim in court, "Hell no. We will not send any more men to prison for refusing to fight this war." At least I wanted to believe in such a possibility.

But while I remained outwardly optimistic, my inner self, the one I kept private even from Mary, began to erect the prison bars around my spirit. I began to withdraw emotionally from the very intimacy Mary and I had hoped to nourish. I had to prepare myself for the isolation prison brings, so I began by isolating myself. Moving out of Colfax House proved most effective. Mary noticed my emotional withdrawal from her and helped me confront the issue. She also had issues dealing with our impending separation, but I will not attempt to speak for her. It is difficult to explain how two people in love can know the best thing for each of them is to be alone, but we came to this realization together, without rancor. We harbored no hard feelings, no anguish, no regrets. We simply accepted that we were on different paths. She did want to stay with me until the actual sentencing, though, and I was thankful she did.

On Monday, January 12, 1970, I reported to Judge Lord's courtroom in Minneapolis. Jack Graham was at my side and would fully represent me from this point on. There were legal motions to be made to keep me out of prison pending appeal, and I didn't want to screw them up acting as my own counsel. But this would be my last chance to convince the judge to tell the nation we were not going to send our young men off to this war anymore. I would have my moment to speak, and I imagined the headlines: "Judge reverses jury verdict: Declares war Immoral." In spite of the hassle I created for him because of my stubborn refusal to play by the rules of the game he had dedicated his life to, I believed Miles Lord liked me and could therefore find some way to keep me out of prison. I was wrong.

Resistance supporters packed the courtroom. The bailiffs had to move some visiting students from Minnetonka High School and Bethel Theological Seminary to seats in front of the rail and in the jury box to accommodate my supporters. Judge Lord's first order of business was to warn them, "You will be removed from the courtroom if there are outbursts of laughter or comments, and I will take your conduct into consideration as an indication of his friends and background when I sentence Mr. Holland." I could clearly see he was not in the mood to rule against the war today.

Assistant U.S. Attorney Ralph Koenig made his case for incarceration and recommended a sentence of two years. I was a bit surprised by this because Dave Gutknecht had received a four-year sentence and George Crocker three years. I was expecting something in the same range. Why was Koenig going soft on me, I wondered.

Jack Graham's turn came next, and he did not disappoint as he proceeded to give one of his eloquent commentaries on the resistance movement. Vietnam, he told the judge, was a military and moral disaster for the United States and it would do to the U.S. what the Russian winter had done to Napoleon and Hitler. "Today you sentence a patriot," Jack told him, "who serves the best interests of his country at grave peril to his own self-interest." Jack later told me he could see "a troubled conscience expressed on Lord's face. His eyes were very sad."

Judge Lord asked if I had anything to say for myself before he handed down his sentence. I couldn't expect to top Jack's eloquence, and I believed Lord's mind was made up before these proceedings began. I chose to keep it simple.

"Today's sentence is not important. We are faced with much greater problems than me going to jail. You, Miles Lord, should consider stepping off the bench and joining us today. You don't stop a war by sentencing draft resisters."

It was Judge Lord's turn now, and my moment of truth.

"I find you to be a decent young man. I have read the presentence report by the probation office and have taken note of your accomplishments. You won athletic letters in football and track four years each and three years in basketball. You served as Junior Editor and Senior Editor of your high school newspaper, Vice-president of the Student Council, and Treasurer of the Luther League. You were co-captain of the debate team and participated in several categories of your high school's forensics competitions. You were a National Merit Scholar and received an American Legion Citizenship award. You also received a four-year journalism scholarship from WCCO-TV.

"You have refused to seek a conscientious objector status. You have chosen instead to set yourself up as some sort of martyr. You have refused to compromise. You may call it patriotism, but I call it very unfortunate for you, Dan Holland. If I were to grant you probation, it would only make a sham of these proceedings because of your work with the Twin Cities Draft Information Center and involvement in the draft resistance movement. Accordingly, it is adjudged that the defendant is hereby committed to the custody of the Attorney General or his authorized representative for imprisonment for a period of two years, defendant to become eligible for parole at such time as the board of parole may determine, consistent with 18 USC 4208 (a) (2)."

Then Judge Lord stood up and started to leave the bench. He looked visibly shaken and overcome with emotion. His voice was audibly trembling at the end of his remarks. Jack told me later that he saw tears in the judge's eyes.

Jack jumped to his feet and called out to the departing Lord, "Your Honor! I wish to make a motion."

Lord turned back to the bench, his voice still a bit unsettled. "Very well, Mr. Graham. What is your motion?"

"I move that this sentence be stayed until the United States Supreme Court delivers its ruling in the David Gutknecht case and the Court of Appeals rules on the George Crocker case."

"So ordered," and his gavel came down.

During the ensuing years Lord would sentence only a few men to prison. David Pence, with whom he had a contentious relationship going back to 1968, he sentenced to a year and a day. Two other less political resisters received six months in prison. Several defendants drew two years' probation if they agreed to two years of civilian work comparable to the work conscientious objectors performed. Then Lord began stating during open court arraignments that any draft resisters could step forward and plead guilty and he would sentence them to probation

David Pence is quoted in Ken Tilsen's book, *Judging the Judges* (North Star Press, 2002), he believed Lord's political buddies were now against the war and the judge was trying to curry their favor. I like to think I had at least a little to do with his change of heart.

40

THE LETTER

January 17, 1970
49,035 Dead

The sun shined brightly on the snow-covered landscape, but it could not warm Minneapolis up to any more than minus 2 degrees Fahrenheit. That's January in Minnesota. It was a perfect day to stay indoors and write some letters, which must have been what my brand-new correspondent decided.

This is what he sent me from Worthington, Minnesota, 175 miles southwest of the Twin Cities:

Dear Daniel:

I have read the account of your conviction on draft evasion charges published in *The Minneapolis Star* of January 14. I was very much intrigued by the following statement attributed to Judge Lord: 'Members of a minority must accept the decisions of the majority.'

Most of the world's atrocities, including the crucifixion of Jesus, can be attributed to majorities. They are generally made up of people highly susceptible to cleverly organized propaganda and either too busy or too lazy to evaluate a cause and to make up their own decisions. The Germans were an intelligent, well-educated, and industrious people, yet they were easily fooled into starting a criminal war by the skillful propaganda of a Hitler and his military clique. What a great moral service the young Germans of that time could have rendered to their own country and to the world by refusing induction.

I am a 79-year-old veteran of World War I. I may not live to see it, but I am confident that the time is not far distant when your courageous stand will be vindicated, perhaps even applauded. God bless you.
—Henry R. Bray

Henry's letter made my day. I treasure it still. Just imagine the horrors of the wars this man fought in and witnessed: WWI, WWII, Korea, and now Vietnam. Rest in Peace, Henry Bray. Rest in Peace.

41

GUTKNECHT DECISION

January 19, 1970
49,053 Dead

Who is frivolous now, Judge Devitt? Almost a year earlier, during a hearing requesting Judge Devitt to continue bail for David Gutknecht while his attorneys appealed to the Supreme Court, following the Eighth Circuit Court of Appeals decision against the legal arguments in the case, Devitt had refused to continue bail because, he said, "The appeal itself is frivolous and there is no chance the Supreme Court will accept this case." He then set a date for David to turn himself in to federal authorities and begin serving his prison sentence.

The date was Friday, March 21, 1969, and it arrived cold and gray and bleak. Dave was a founding father of the Twin Cities draft resistance movement, and his leadership style was highly regarded throughout movement circles for his intelligence, commitment, and sincerity. Dave was not a flashy public speaker, but he drew you in with a quiet charisma resonating with honesty, sense of purpose, and an immediacy that heightened the importance of his message. He was easy to believe and to believe in.

Probably 200 people showed up for his farewell at the new federal building. Speakers praised Dave's courage and commitment. Songs were sung in honor of his sacrifice. Then suddenly, and most unexpectedly, Chester Bruvold, Dave's attorney, grabbed the megaphone and blurted out to the crowd, "I have just this moment received a call from Justice Byron White of the Supreme Court granting a continuance of Dave's bail while the court decides if it will take his case. David Gutknecht will remain a free man!"

Pandemonium broke out. I do not remember ever experiencing such elation, such overwhelming joy. We closed the TCDIC offices and spent the rest of the day in celebration, the likes of which I have never seen again.

Then the waiting game began. It would be the last week of April before the Supreme Court announced it would hear the Gutknecht case. Oral arguments were made in November. And then, on January 19, 1970, the Supreme Court of the United States of America decided in favor of David Gutknecht. I had resented Judge Devitt from the moment the word "frivolous" came out of his mouth. How dare Devitt trivialize all of the lives at stake in these cases? Now the Supreme Court proved him more than wrong, perhaps even frivolous himself. (But enough about Judge Devitt. I'll get over it eventually. Just give me a couple more years.)

The morning of January 19th, Dave came into the office attempting to look nonchalant, as if nothing out of the ordinary had happened to him yet. But the ear-to-ear grin was a dead giveaway, and he had to give it up almost immediately. A reporter from *The New York Times* had awakened him with a phone call that morning to ask how he felt about his victory in the Supreme Court. This was the first Dave heard of it. In typical Dave Gutknecht style, he downplayed the importance of his own case for the reporter, calling it "a limited victory for the draft resistance movement." There were, of course, hundreds of thousands of American soldiers still in harm's way, and much work to do before peace would prevail.

Dave was happy, though. He did not have prison staring him directly in the face anymore. But he was also realistic. The Supreme Court decided the case on narrow legal technicalities. Essentially, the Court ruled that when Congress passed the Selective Service Act, it did not intend for the local draft boards to have the authority to "punish" war protesters by putting their names at the head of the call list, ahead even of volunteers, for infractions of regulations established by the Selective Service System. Instead, Congress specifically mandated punishments be administered by the courts for infractions of Selective Service regulations. Returning or destroying one's draft card, the court ruled, constituted protected free speech. In addition, since the "delinquency" status did not allow for any appeal by the draft registrant, the procedure was ruled an unconstitutional denial of due process. Well over 30,000 men had their draft status and even draft convictions and sentences reversed as a result. (The decision written for the majority by Justice William O. Douglas is too detailed to reprint here, but it is well worth finding on-line for those who are interested.) Dave understood that while he was free now, he would soon be drafted again, by the book this time, which is exactly what happened.

I, on the other hand, was just as happy as I could be. I knew the ruling in Dave's case would be grounds to overturn my conviction. I also knew Dave could be drafted again because now there was a lottery to establish the order of call and Dave's birthday had come up as number 43, but my own birthday came up number 347. I knew they would never draft that far down the list. I was free. The self-constructed interior prison walls I had been building around my emotional center began to melt away immediately.

I called Jack Graham to see what we needed to do. He had just heard the news and was already preparing a motion to present to Judge Lord. A lengthy process then ensued. Because my case was currently in the hands of the Eighth Circuit Court of Appeals, a motion had to be made to return the case to the District Court, based on the ruling of the Supreme Court in the Gutknecht case, in order for Judge Lord to have jurisdiction over the matter once again. Shuffling the paperwork would take almost three months, but my day would come.

42

THE BEAVER 55

February 28, 1970, 1970
49,833 Dead

I was out of town for the whole weekend. I really was. But nobody in Minneapolis believed me. Not my co-workers at TCDIC. Not the FBI. Nobody. I left Friday afternoon, drove all the way to Milwaukee by myself, and returned late Sunday night, again by myself. But if I needed an alibi, I had at least a dozen friends in Milwaukee who would testify I was there from Friday night to Sunday night. I had gone there specifically to see Lynne, whom I had met at the Milwaukee 14 trial, but had also become friends with all the people who lived in the Muck House on Milwaukee's East side on the corner of Thomas and Murray.

When I left for work on Monday morning, the car was parked in front of the house (I was still house sitting for the Roths' and driving their Bug), and as I pulled away from the curb, I noticed in my rear view mirror a car a little ways behind me pulled out at the same time. Not too unusual, I just noted it as part of my surrounding traffic. But when I turned right at the very first corner and the car behind followed, I felt just a hint of suspicion, so I turned right again. Suspicion confirmed: I was being followed. A third right turn pegged these two guys as FBI. Why were they following me? I really had no idea. But now I was at the fourth corner and a right turn put me right back in front of the house where we had started our little journey around the block. My original parking space was still vacant, of course, and I pulled the Bug in, got out, waved to the Feds, and walked the two

The Minnesota 8 in 1970. Back row from left to right: Pete Simmons, Bill Tilton, Frank Kronke. Front row: Chuck Turchick, Mike Therriault, Brad Beneke, Don Olson. Photo by Cheryl Walsh Bellville.

blocks up to Lake Street. The Feds pretended not to see me as they drove by, and then I spotted them again when I got up to the corner of Lake and Fremont. Are you guys going to follow me hitchhiking, I thought? I could take you on a trip all over the Twin Cities and never go anywhere. How much fun could we have going in circles all day? But then they pulled away and left. When I arrived at the office, there they were, parked across the street. Duh. Where did these guys think I was going to go?

I climbed the stairs to the office. Dave was already there, and the coffee was brewed. "An odd thing happened this morning," I said, just making conversation as I poured a cup of coffee. "The FBI tried to follow me to work, so I ditched the car at home and hitched. Now they're sitting in their car, right across the street."

"That's not odd at all after what happened this weekend," Dave said.

"Why? What happened? I was in Milwaukee all weekend," I reminded him. Naturally, I had told everyone I was going to Milwaukee before I left.

"Oh, right, of course. I knew that." Then he tossed the front page of the newspaper across his desk to me.

"Raiders Damage Draft Records in Twin Cities" read the front-page headline. I looked up at Dave and he was smiling at me. I looked back at the article and read out loud, "Large quantities of draft records were destroyed or damaged late Saturday or early Sunday at the state Selective Service office and at local draft offices in downtown St. Paul and Minneapolis. Officials said they had no suspects or leads."

"So thaaaat's why they were following me," I said. "I had no idea this happened."

"Oh, right," Dave said. "How could you know? You were out of town aaalll weekend."

"I really was, Dave. You know I support these actions, but I wasn't in on this one." Dave Gutknecht did not support the draft board raids, and he made very cogent arguments about crossing the line from nonviolence to violence when it came down to property destruction. I agreed with him to a point. I did not support the damaging or burning or bombing of buildings. I did not even support trashing typewriters as some raiders did so they couldn't be used to fill out draft forms. But I considered draft files themselves to be instruments of death with no useful purpose, and I supported their destruction. I believed destroying draft files could save lives.

So the FBI guys sat in their car across the street from our office all day. I wonder if they found anything out by just sitting there. Meanwhile, another FBI agent called our office and asked for me by name. I took the call for amusement purposes only.

"Can you account for your whereabouts during the past weekend?" he asked.

"You've got to be kidding. You don't really think I'm going to answer any of your questions, do you?"

"Where were you on Saturday night?"

"Now this is just silly," I said. "I will not answer any questions. Period."

"We can bring you in for questioning, you know."

"That would be a waste of everybody's time. But go ahead and do what you've gotta do." Since I knew I had not been a part of the raid, there was no need for me to mention my multiple alibis and sic the FBI on my Milwaukee friends unless I was actually charged with a crime.

Only one person besides me even knew about any involvement I may have had prior to the raid. I have never told anyone this before because these actions are and must be kept secret, but I was recruited to take part in this raid. I attended a weekend retreat out of state hosted by some of the biggest names in the draft board raid movement, but in the end I decided not to participate. At the time of the retreat I was still facing a prison term for refusing induction, and I did not relish the thought of adding additional prison time to my already crowded schedule.

Some time after the retreat one person who would be my only contact approached me regarding the special access I had as a draft counselor to the draft board offices. Quite often I would receive written permission from someone I was counseling to examine his draft file at the draft board. It was so common for draft boards to make clerical and procedural errors that this was an excellent stalling tactic to gain time for a potential draftee to re-qualify for a lost deferment. My contact asked if I would make maps of the interiors of the draft board offices: every desk, chair, office machine, file cabinet, window, and door. Now there was a risk I was willing to take, a clandestine operation right under the eyes of the draft boards clerical staff. Over the next several weeks I made detailed maps of all three offices and cased the buildings inside and out. I was not told who would be in the group or when the action would take place, and I was assured no one in the group would be told of my participation. It was purely coincidental I happened to be out of town on the weekend of the raid, as I had no advance warning of when the action would take place. But being away all weekend did make it appear to my friends as if I participated in the action.

Many previous raiders had chosen to stay and defend their actions in court, but none of those defenses had been successful. More and more the draft board raids were hit and run. A group calling themselves the Beaver 55 conducted this raid. The same name had been used to claim credit for actions in Michigan, Indiana, and Illinois. Over 300 raids on draft boards were conducted before the end of the war. Several rallies would be held in support of the Beaver 55 in the coming weeks, including a huge rock and roll event at Coffman Memorial Union on the U of M campus, at which 3,000 people signed a statement declaring they were members of the Beaver 55. I proudly signed on the dotted line. The action crippled Minnesota's ability to meet its draft quotas. No charges were ever filed in the case.

The following July, by which time I was gone from Minnesota (real gone), a group of raiders who became known as the Minnesota 8 attempted to raid the draft board offices in Alexandria, Little Falls, and Winona, but FBI agents alerted by an informant arrested them as they entered those offices. Unknown members of the same group successfully struck Wabasha the same night and destroyed all of the draft files there.

Arrested at Winona were Don Olson, Peter Simmons, and Brad Beneke; at Alexandria William Tilton, Chuck Turchick, and Cliff Ulen; at Little Falls Michael Therriault and Frank Kronke.

Cliff Ulen pleaded guilty and received probation. The other seven men chose to go to trial in order to make their moral and legal arguments against the war and the draft and in favor of their moral and legal responsibilities to act. All of them were convicted and sentenced to five years, and each of them ended up serving between twenty and twenty-four months. At their trial later in the year, the group's lawyer, Ken Tilsen, called Daniel Ellsberg as a witness. Ellsberg was replacing Noam Chomsky who had been unable to rearrange his schedule in order to testify at the trial. Dave Dellinger, a leading antiwar proponent, had recommended Ellsberg, telling Tilsen he could not reveal his testimony ahead of time, but it would really shake things up.

Daniel Ellsberg had been looking for a legal way to release the top-secret internal Defense Department's 43-volume history of U.S. involvement in Vietnam, which became known as the Pentagon Papers and detailed the lies told to the American people and the Congress. Through a set of skillfully posed questions by Ken Tilsen, Ellsberg intended to reveal the Pentagon Papers on the witness stand, thereby protecting himself from prosecution for releasing them. But the Judge suspected something and, without knowing exactly what was coming, halted Ellsberg's testimony, threatening Tilsen with contempt if he tried again to present testimony insinuating the government had lied. Six months later Ellsberg would release the Pentagon Papers to *The New York Times*.

It is interesting to note the very first raid on a draft board during the Vietnam war era occurred in Elk River, Minnesota, in the spring of 1966 and became known as the Big Lake One in honor of the hometown of the lone raider, Barry Bondhus. Barry and his ten brothers, with the support and supervision of their father, Tom Bondhus, collected their own feces in buckets for two weeks. Barry then schlepped the buckets to his draft board in his pick-up truck and unceremoniously dumped the contents into the file drawers rendering the files useless. His action did not immediately gain national attention the way the Baltimore Four did a year later, when Father Phillip Berrigan and friends Tom Lewis, James Mengel, and David Eberhardt poured their own blood on draft files, or six months after that when Phil and his brother Daniel Berrigan, also a Catholic priest, were joined by seven others as they destroyed draft files with homemade napalm in Catonsville, Maryland. Phil and Daniel were both born in Minnesota, adding to the state's rich pantheon of peacemakers and activists. Indeed, if we count the 3,000 people who signed the statement claiming responsibility for the Beaver 55, no other state even comes close.

43

My Conviction Vacated

April 2, 1970
50,056 Dead

The sweet taste of freedom. This was a happy day for me, and several of my closest friends came along to celebrate my final day in court. Jack Graham was by my side, of course, and we sat again at the same table as the Assistant U.S. Attorney and his associate.

"You are a lucky young man," Koenig said to me.

"So are you," I said back to him. He looked confused.

"All rise," the bailiff commanded. "The Honorable Miles Lord presiding."

I remained seated as the judge entered the courtroom and sat down at his bench without making eye contact with anyone. He kept his gaze on some papers he was shuffling as the bailiff intoned the case by number and name. Then Lord read from his prepared statement.

"The above matter having been remanded by the United States Court of Appeals for the Eighth Circuit pursuant to Gutknecht v. U.S., 90 S.Ct. 506, for action by this Court,

"IT IS NOW ORDERED that the judgment entered as of January 12, 1969 [sic], herein is in all things vacated, the indictment is dismissed and the defendant is discharged." As Jack and I hugged, the judge got up and left the courtroom. I left just as quickly in the arms of my laughing friends.

In the ten weeks since the Supreme Court's Gutknecht decision, my outlook on life had completely turned around. I was no longer isolating myself within the prison walls of my own psyche. Now I saw the world as wide

184 ◆ DANIEL HOLLAND

open before me. Having spent the last two years working full time to bring America back on the right course, I felt a passionate yearning to explore this vast nation and discover what the people outside of my tight-knit circle were really like. I did not have a plan and I did not want a plan for this pilgrimage. I wanted an open-ended journey of discovery. I just wanted to go and to witness. I wanted to let my life unfold. I would make no rules to limit my experience, nor would I harbor any preconceived notions about how this undertaking would turn out.

I did have to take the first step, though, before I could follow through with the next one. I had decided to begin in Denver. Bob and Ed, both friends and supporters from Minneapolis, were going to college in Denver, and when they heard my plan to explore America, they invited me to begin by visiting them. Martha and Marty Roth had just returned from Mexico and surprised me with a tip of fifty dollars for the house sitting. This was more than enough for a one-way plane ticket to Denver, and thus my quest began.

Mary took the bus out to the airport with me. This would be our real goodbye. While we sat waiting for my boarding call, we daydreamed about a future without war. Then it was time to go. As I started down the jetway, I paused and turned back for one last look. Mary was standing there with both of her hands over her heart, a sad little smile on her face, her head tilted just a bit to the left with her hair hanging down over her right eye. I tried to make my last look expressionless, but I don't know if I did. Maybe there was a tear in my eye. Then I turned and walked away. I would not see her again for 44 years. But I never forgot the lessons we learned together.

44

THE KENT STATE KILLINGS

May 4, 1970
51,290 Dead

Arriving in Denver I felt a mile high in body, mind, and spirit. Each step I took would be into an uncharted future. Let the world unfurl before me. My excitement must have been evident in my eyes, perhaps even my aura, as I seemed to be floating through the airport crowd as if on a cloud. When my feet finally did touch the ground, I found myself in a dorm room at the tiny private college attended by Bob and Ed. They were the only two students who had stayed on campus during Easter break, so we basically had the place to ourselves, except for the young priest in charge of the dorms. He stopped by in the afternoon to check on his two students. Naturally enough, he wanted to know my history, my reason for being there.

As I related in detail my story of draft resistance, defending myself in court, and then suddenly finding myself free, I could sense the padre's style of relating to his students was to be just one of the guys. He wanted to win respect through camaraderie rather than authority. Clearly this must have seemed the easiest, perhaps even the wisest, way for him given how close in age he was to his students. He reacted to my tale with enthusiasm. He turned out to be completely sympathetic. He opposed the war. He admired the resistance. I concluded my narrative with, "Now I'm on a quest. Where it will take me, I just don't know."

"Well, if you need a place to stay until you put your feet on the ground," he said, "you can have a room right here. We have a couple of unoccupied dorm rooms. You'll even get clean linens every Friday. No charge."

Wow. I was not anticipating such generosity, but I thanked him and accepted. Since my quest had no blueprint, I was free to let it unfold as it would. I had my sights set on Berkeley, yes, but I had no timetable to adhere to. Free housing was an opportunity worth exploring. Bob and Ed and I spent the weekend listening to music (they were both musicians) and telling tales of people we knew in Minneapolis. On Sunday, the rest of the students started filtering back to resume their studies for the final month of the school year.

Student life returned to normal on Monday morning, but for me there was no normal. I had the address and phone number of the draft resistance office in Denver, but when I called, the number was disconnected. I then made my way from campus to the resistance office address by thumb. When I arrived, I met one young woman there packing up the last of their files into boxes. As was happening across the country, support for draft counseling services had dwindled with the advent of the lottery, and they didn't have the money to keep their office open anymore. I introduced myself and helped this lonely survivor finish packing up and move the boxes into the house she shared with the last of the Denver cadre not in prison. They would continue to provide what support they could from their home, but it was sad to see their infrastructure fade like this.

At the resistance house I met another woman who was about five or six years older than me. As we talked, it became evident we knew many of the same people, most of them participants in draft board raids. She asked me to come upstairs with her. I followed her to the third-floor attic room where she was staying. We sat on a mattress by the window looking out on the street and shared stories about our mutual friends. Then she told me she had participated in a recent raid. She was part of a "hit and run" raid, the same tactic used by the Beaver 55, but the FBI had come looking for her for questioning, so she disappeared. Just then we were startled by the flashing red lights of a police car pulling up right in front of the house.

"Wow. This could be it for me," she said.

We watched as two cops got out of their car and walked around a car parked right in front of the house, checking it out and looking inside. The car did not belong to anyone associated with the house and that eased our fears a little bit. The cops got back in their car and sat there for who knows how long. Then they just left.

We continued watching out the window until it was dark outside and then briefly left our attic room to procure a bottle of wine. There ensued some laughing, some handholding, some tenderness shared until a faint light began to appear in the East. I must have fallen asleep then because I remember waking up and she was gone. I have never seen or heard of her again.

Using my thumb, I made my way back to the campus. I did not yet feel compelled to leave. By default, I guess, I simply began to live the student life along with my friends. Picking my favorites from Bob's and Ed's schedules, I started attending classes with them, always sitting in the back but waiting for, expecting, an instructor to question my presence. It never happened. I was taking notes in class and even writing papers although I never turned them in. That would have brought unwanted attention. Perhaps this was just the experience I needed, to not be on call for the revolution every single moment.

Then one day four of my "classmates" joined me in my dorm room to smoke a little pot. I don't even remember whose weed it was, but my room was the one with no roommate, so it had some privacy. Somebody rolled a joint, and after it had gone around a couple of times, there was a loud knocking on the door. The friendly young priest's voice came booming through: "Open this door right now!"

My friends were immediately gasping as if it had never occurred to them this could happen. I told them I was going to open the door and they should all just leave and walk down the hall and out of the building. I would talk to the priest, and no matter what he said, they should just keep walking. I didn't know what I would say yet, but I hoped I would be able to take the blame and spare them the embarrassment, or even worse, disciplinary action.

I swung the door open, and the guys hotfooted their way down the hall just as I had instructed. Then I stepped into the hall, pulled the door closed, and faced the priest. I decided I would let him start the conversation, as I still had not figured out what I was going to say. He glared at me.

"We don't allow people to smoke marijuana here."

I returned his gaze but tried to look dispassionate, and then the words just came to me.

"They don't allow people to smoke marijuana anywhere," I replied calmly, which pretty much seemed to wrap up any debate we might have about the subject. I turned and walked down the hallway myself. As I walked away, I expected to hear him say, "I want you out of this room by the end of the day and off this campus for good," but he didn't say a word. He continued to treat me with kindness and respect for the remaining two weeks of the semester, and he never brought the subject up again. None of the students who had been in the room was ever disciplined or reprimanded. Imagine my surprise forty-four years later when Colorado became the first state to legalize recreational marijuana.

Of course, when the semester did end, my future opened before me again. Berkeley was a destination I'd had in mind from the beginning, because I wanted to experience the birthplace of the Free Speech Movement. Steve had invited some of his college friends, and me, to come to his family's home in Los Angeles, where his family's connections could help everyone find a summer job. I was just happy for the ride to the West Coast. We piled seven people into two cars and instead of taking I-70 straight to LA, we took I-25 south to I-40 because we wanted to stop at the Grand Canyon, which none of us but Steve had ever seen. The view was definitely worth the few extra hours in the car, and I know it gave me a sense of the grandeur of our nation.

We drove all night and then all day before arriving late at night on May 4th. Exhausted, we just collapsed on couches and floors and slept until late the next morning. Always the early riser, I was the first one up and headed for the kitchen, hoping for coffee. I found Steve's mother there, looking very somber, and introduced myself. Without saying a word, she pushed the front page of the morning's *Los Angeles Times* across the kitchen table, and I saw the headline: "Troops Kill Four Students in Antiwar Riot at Ohio College." I was stunned. Mrs. K was stunned. We had just this moment met each other, and she knew nothing about me except I was one of the six friends from college Steve had brought home for the summer. We had remained out of touch with the outside world on our thirty-hour drive from Denver, so we had not heard about the Kent State killings the day before. Mrs. K and I tried to find some words to comfort each other, but it was an impossible task. All we could find was dismay.

"I'm leaving for Berkeley today," I told her. I knew that's where the action I wanted to be part of would happen.

She immediately tried to dissuade me. She was a loving mother and caring person who did not want to be witness to any more killing. She warned me about what California's governor had said just three weeks earlier at a meeting of the Council of California Growers. Ronald Reagan, Governor of California then and the pride of the Republican Party even today, answering a question about the People's Park protests at Berkeley, said, "If it takes a bloodbath, let's get it over with. No more appeasement." I don't know how crass you can get, but that has got to be pretty damn close to the limit.

I tried to assure Mrs. K I was quite experienced in protest tactics and would be able to protect myself. I knew she wasn't buying it, though. As we talked about the Kent State killings and the Berkeley protests and just plain got to know each other, the rest of the traveling crew gradually drifted in from their slumbers. Each of them in turn reacted with shock to the head-lines, and the discussion had to begin anew. Once everyone was awake and informed, I asked Steve to give me a ride to the nearest freeway entrance ramp. I had to get to Berkeley.

Steve, of course, wasn't going to just drop me off at the nearest ramp. "You'll never get a ride out of town from there," he said. "I'll take you to a place where you're certain to get a good ride." Mrs. K cut off the end of a cardboard box and fashioned me a sign reading simply "SF," and away we went, the whole crew in two cars, just to see me off on the highway.

There I was, standing at the entrance to the freeway farther away from Minnesota than I had ever been, alone, with my little cardboard sign and my backpack with my pillow tied to the top, yet full of hope. It was early afternoon when my friends had dropped me off, and as the sun was setting, I began to wonder if I would ever get off this godforsaken ramp. Finally, a car slowed and pulled to the side to offer me a ride. I ran over to the pas-senger side of the vehicle and opened the door.

"Where you heading? "I asked the driver, a young man about my age.

"Not far," he said, "but I can sure get you to a better spot than this one."

I didn't need convincing. "Get me out of here," I said as I climbed in. I will not do a rundown of the multiple rides I got "to a better spot" over the next three days, but three days is how long it took me to hitchhike out of LA.

The breakthrough ride came when three Latino guys in a pickup truck stopped and told me I would have better luck taking Highway 1 up the coast. Since I had had no luck at all thus far, I accepted their ride, hoisted my backpack into the bed of the truck, and climbed in after it. After a wild ride out to Malibu, they dropped me on a two-lane road where I could even walk north if I wanted to. It had to be twenty or more rides later and most of a day when I arrived in the Bay Area and well after midnight when I landed in Berkeley.

I had never been to Berkeley before, but I had looked at some maps to get an idea of the layout. When my last ride dropped me off on University Avenue, I knew it would take me to the campus if I just kept walking to the East. It was late at night, and the town was pretty quiet, a few cars driving by but no pedestrian traffic at all. I had barely set foot on the campus when a University cop car pulled up out of nowhere and activated its flashing emergency lights. I stopped in my tracks, turned to face the squad car, and as the first officer exited his vehicle, I let my backpack fall from my shoulders. The second officer got out of the car but remained standing next to it with his hand on his weapon.

"Looks like you just got to town," the first cop said, nudging my backpack with the toe of his boot.

"I did."

"You come for the protests?"

"I'm on a quest. It's a long story."

"You'll have to tell me some time, but here's a good story for you. We've been having a lot of protests on campus, and there's word out someone may try to bring explosives in. You got any explosives in your pack?"

"I can promise you I do not."

"Then you won't mind if I check, will you?"

"Correct me if I'm wrong, but don't you need a search warrant?"

"Here's how it works: You grant me permission to search your pack and if there is nothing illegal in there, you can go on your way. Or, you refuse permission to search your pack, I take you in on suspicion, and your pack gets searched at headquarters. We're gonna search your pack."

"Well, let's get it over with right now."

I knew there were no explosives, weapons, or drugs to be found, so this seemed the quickest way to end our encounter. We chatted pleasantly as he untied my pillow from the top, unstrapped the upper flap, and one-by-one pulled every item I owned from the pack and carefully placed each of them on the ground. I sat on the sidewalk and watched. The second cop came over and asked for my ID so he could check for wants and warrants. I handed him my Minnesota driver's license.

"You're clean," the first cop said when he finished unpacking me. "Enjoy your stay in Berkeley."

I sat by my belongings and watched him walk back to his cruiser. In a couple of minutes cop number two returned with my driver's license.

"You're good to go," he says, "and I recommend that's what you do."

As I sat there amidst all my worldly possessions (a few clothes, notebooks, tooth brush, hair brush, too many books), my best guess was if I packed up all my stuff and started walking again, the next cop who spotted me would repeat the procedure. So I stayed put until dawn.

As Berkeley slowly came to life, I packed up and headed for Telegraph Avenue in search of coffee. It was easy in those days to make friends, and I quickly fell in with some like-minded people I met at the coffeehouse and Moe's Books, my two most frequent hangouts.

The Berkeley campus was in full support of the nationwide student strike that had shut down over 450 campuses when more than 4 million students and 350,000 faculty members refused to go about business as usual in response to the invasion of Cambodia and the subsequent Kent State killings. There were daily demonstrations starting on Sproul Plaza spilling into the streets, with cops from all over wearing riot gear and ready to pounce. Then on May 15 Mississippi State Troopers killed two students and wounded twelve more during antiwar protests at Jackson State College. The weekend after the Kent State killings saw 100,000 protesters massing in front of the White House and another 150,000 demonstrators rallied in San Francisco. Thirty campus ROTC buildings across the country were either burned or bombed. The tension in the air was thick. We believed the revolution was finally under way.

It is worth mentioning what Henry Kissinger wrote in his memoirs (*White House Years*, pp. 511–513) about this time: "Campus unrest and violence overtook the Cambodian operation itself as the major issue before the public. Washington took on the character of a besieged city . . . .. The very fabric of government was falling apart."

I also had a personal problem I was trying to resolve at the time. Just before I left Denver, my mother had sent me a letter with my brand-new draft card. My local draft board had sent it to the last known address they had on file for me, which was my mother's address. It was burning a hole in my pocket. I knew I couldn't hold on to it, but I had not yet figured out a properly righteous and politically compelling method of disposing of it. Of course, I could just return it to the draft board. Because they would not be able to draft me at all with the lottery in place now, and my number way too high, their only recourse would be to refer the matter back to the United States Attorney's office. He was unlikely to prosecute me for failure to carry the card since his calendar was already more than fifty percent draft cases, so that option didn't seem like it would have much impact. Only a handful of resisters were ever prosecuted for returning or burning a draft card. Local draft boards had accused over 209,000 men of Selective Service System violations. An estimated 360,000 resisters, including 250,000 who never registered, were never brought into the legal system. A total of 8,750 men were convicted of Selective Service felonies. Not that I was anxious to go back to court and face prison again, but I needed to get rid of the draft card and make a statement doing it. Then Neil Young came to my rescue.

When Crosby, Stills, Nash, and Young came out with the song "Ohio" in response to the Kent State shooting, I knew immediately what I would do. The song was being played every hour on a San Francisco radio station, and I only had to hear the song a couple of times to get the lyrics written down. I sent them, along with my new draft card, to Judge Miles Lord.

I included a short letter with the lyrics and draft card, but I do not remember what I wrote. However, I do still have Judge Lord's reply in my possession. Here it is in its entirety:

Dear Mr. Holland:
I am returning to you herewith your draft card which you enclosed with your letter of May 20, 1970.
The answer to your inquiry in that letter is "No".
Very truly yours.
Miles W. Lord.

I can only speculate what my "inquiry" was, but knowing myself as I do, I expect it was something on the order of, "You don't expect me to walk around with this thing in my pocket, do you?" I have attempted to contact the retired Judge Lord during the writing of this memoir, both through the courts and through his daughter's law office in Minneapolis, but they have chosen not to respond. I had hoped he might still have my letter in his personal papers and share it with me, but we'll just have to go with my speculation here.

I was making a political statement by sending my draft card to Judge Lord, the man who had tried to send me to prison for two years. All he had to do was walk down the hallway to the U. S. Attorney's office and hand him my letter as evidence of a crime. Because he chose not to do so is proof enough for me that he had indeed turned the corner in his opinion about the war and those of us who were striving to end it.

(It is with sadness I report Judge Miles W. Lord died on December 10, 2016, at the age of 97, before I had secured a publisher for this manuscript. Rest in peace, Your Honor. Rest in peace.)

After I mailed the letter to Lord, I walked up Telegraph Avenue to the University. It was drizzling with unusually low gray clouds rolling just above the building tops, catching the peak of the campanile, obscuring the clock. I made my way through the sidewalk food carts strewn along Bancroft Way, cut across Sproul Plaza, and followed Strawberry Creek through the Eucalyptus Grove to University Avenue where I stuck out my thumb.

I would spend the next two years hitchhiking from the West Coast to the East Coast, through the Deep South, and all around the Midwest with frequent treks back to the West Coast, all in search of the Real America. But that's another story.

Afterword

January 10, 2019
Too Many People Have Died

Deep in the cargo holds of ocean-going freighters lurk some of the se-crets of global economics. Back in the late Seventies, I worked as a long-shoreman in the Port of Milwaukee. Most of our cargo was Food for Peace Program milled grain in 50-pound bags, occasionally 50-kilo sacks of flour, and sometimes 55-gallon drums of edible oil. It was physically demanding labor with damn good pay. But from time-to-time there would be cargo I did not care to work, raw cow hides being the first on that list. Hides come cut whole from the animal, folded into a bundle, and cross-tied with twine to provide a handle. They are heavy, smelly, slimy, and often covered with maggots. Because we had a strong union (the International Longshore-men's Association), we had the option to "check out," or leave the job at the end of any four hour shift, provided there were replacements available in the hiring hall, so any time I got stuck on hides, I checked out. Once, when I was leaving a Russian freighter at the noon break knowing I would not return, I passed the ship's captain on the deck (not an unusual occurrence), and asked him, "What're you going to do with all these cow hides?" He looked me right in the eye and said, "Make army boots."

On another bright, sun-shining day, I found myself in the hold of a ship bound for Israel unloading pallets of 105mm brass artillery shell cas-ings. Just the casings without the charge or the projectile, but still, a sense of the macabre settled in on us as we steadily surrounded ourselves with thousands of artillery shells knowing they would be assembled into live weapons upon reaching their destination, then fired at living people in the Gaza Strip, the West Bank, Lebanon, Syria, Egypt. I checked out. I couldn't stop the shipment from leaving the port. I couldn't stop the wars that were sure to flare up in the Middle East. All I could do was keep my own handprints off the bombs. A week later we were loading camouflaged fire trucks headed for Egypt. That's right, American manufacturers were doing business with both sides of the conflict in pursuit of the almighty dollar. No conscience necessary.

Global arms sales in 2016 totaled $374.8 billion, and the U. S. share of the world arms market reached 58 percent. To maintain this level of arms sales requires the weapons be fired after deployment to their respective conflict zones and then replenished. It is also necessary the weapons be updated, redesigned, and used again. I think this is the very definition of a vicious circle. The managers of today's war machine, which include the corporate oligarchs whose money controls the politicians, generals, and strategists, have no incentive to eliminate war. Profit is their only incentive.

On April 16, 1953, just three months after he took office and shortly after the death of Joseph Stalin, President Dwight D. Eisenhower gave his Chance for Peace speech in which he said, "Every gun that is made, every warship launched, every rocket fired signifies, in the final sense, a theft from those who hunger and are not fed, those who are cold and are not clothed." He went on to list in detail all the schools, hospitals, power plants, and highways that would not be built because of the money diverted to military spending. After eight years as president, Eisenhower had been unable to stem the arms race and left office with this dire warning: "We must guard against the acquisition of unwarranted influence . . . by the military-industrial complex. The potential for the disastrous rise of misplaced power exists, and will persist." He was right about that.

Would I resist the draft all over again in today's world? I would in a heartbeat. I remain as convinced as ever that individuals must be responsible for their own actions, by which I mean we do not have the luxury to claim, "I was just following orders." When we pull the trigger to fire the weapon or when we push the button to launch the missile, we are making an individual choice to commit an act of war. War is a crime against humanity. It is incumbent upon each of us, then, to refuse participation.

Probably there are a few individuals from the resistance who may now regret their past decisions, but many more people who supported the Vietnam War have come to understand the magnitude of their mistake. I remain steadfastly opposed to war. I still believe an essential ingredient for peace is for individual people to make moral choices about how to conduct their own lives rather than leaving those decisions to the government or the generals. The war in Vietnam was finally halted, in part, because millions of people resisted, protested, and demonstrated.

The Vietnam War could never have been fought at the levels it reached without the draft to facilitate its need for bodies. While the volunteer army we have now is one check we possess to prevent our government from waging foreign wars with no real national security threat, this alone is not enough, as the wars in Afghanistan and Iraq have shown us. The volunteer soldiers of today are forced to serve three and four tours of duty in war zones as recruitment levels decline in the face of these unpopular conflicts, resulting in higher rates of death, injury, and permanent disability. Lack of a draft, some argue, also provides incentive for keeping the minimum wage low, and makes sure that a job in the military is an attractive option for many in our underpaid workforce.

I will never be a brilliant military strategist, I grant you that, but I am capable of perceiving the ineptitude of the military and political strategists who have failed to resolve the conflict in Afghanistan for eighteen years and counting. Once again, it is incumbent upon us as individuals to hold the government accountable. Relying on a few days of voting every few years is not sufficient. We must be in the streets and in the faces of the officials elected to represent us, not decide for us.

A standing army may be necessary to defend our country from attack but spreading our unique brand of militarism across the globe seems to perpetuate the culture of war, not promote the peace. Consider this picture: The United States has over 800 military bases in 70 foreign countries; Russia, France, and Great Britain have a combined 30 foreign military bases; China has one. Our government may think we have every right to declare ourselves the Wyatt Earp of the world and to gun down the bad guys at every O. K. Corral we can find, but the rest of the world may see a blustering bully intent on controlling the flow of natural resources and economic development. Again, to maintain such a high level of military presence throughout the world, the government is going to need bodies, and I think they've found a way.

Congress has created The National Commission on Military, National, and Public Service (with the euphemistic website of Inspire2Serve.gov) "to review the military selective service process and consider ways to increase participation by all Americans in military, national, and public service." What this commission is trying to say here is that the courts are likely to rule the current selective service system registration requirement unconstitutional because it does not include women even though the military has now opened all military positions, including combat and Special Forces, to women. (A federal district court judge in Texas ruled in February 2019 that the all-male draft is unconstitutional; the case will likely take years to resolve and could well end up before the Supreme Court.) Therefore, the military is going to need a means by which it can force people to serve there and in other professions they deem necessary to national security during any emergency, real or self-created. By conflating "military service" with "national and public service," the Commission seeks, by their own words, the "means to foster a greater attitude and ethos of service among American youth." I take this to mean a greater acceptance of compulsory service by suggesting you may have some choice in the type of service. I recommend you remain wary of any such gimmick. The goal here will be to compel service in the military, including especially medical professionals, or whatever defense industries are critical to any war effort.

While the latest numbers may indicate a significant decline in worldwide war-related deaths, making our current era the most peaceful time in more than a century, the numbers are still too high. Spend a few hours on the Internet and you can identify more than 60 countries involved in more than 700 armed conflicts. It will be argued by some that this is our natural condition because Homo Sapiens is trapped by its genetics in an inescapable determinism we cannot undo while we inexorably hurtle toward our own destruction. They will argue that our technological capabilities to build increasingly more powerful weapons of mass destruction far outpace our ability to control our basest nature. This is essentially an argument for doing nothing to stop the ongoing killing.

But maybe, just maybe, we as individuals can break the cycle by taking individual responsibility. Maybe, just maybe, we will harness our considerable imaginations to create powerful mechanisms for a more equitable, and therefore less combative, world.

This is my call to resist. Go ahead and vote, protest, demonstrate, write letters, and organize, all of which is important work. But do not put your body in their hands to do their bidding for war and profit. One by one, you and I together, we are the paths to peace.

#   #   #

Comparing notes and sharing memories with the old gang prior to beginning the writing process. From left to right, George Crocker, Don Olson, Bill Tilton, Daniel Holland, Pete Simmons, Dave Gutknecht, and David Luce on July 21, 2014.

BIBLIOGRAPHY

I list here many of the books that influenced my early learning along with several more recent texts that are relevant to the discussion at hand. This is not intended to be a comprehensive bibliography but rather a starting point for those who may be interested in further exploring ideas of nonviolent protest, civil disobedience, militarism, war, and social justice. If readers were to just scratch the surface of this list, they would be led to hundreds of fascinating and engaging ideas, concepts, and proposals for understanding this world and making it a safer, saner place.

Appy, Christian G. *American Reckoning: The Vietnam War and Our National Identity*. New York: Viking Penguin, 2015.

Bacevich, Andrew J. *The New American Militarism: How Americans Are Seduced by War*. New York: Oxford University Press, Inc., 2005.

Baldwin, James. *The Fire Next Time*. New York: Dial Press, 1963.

Bingham, Clara. *Witness to the Revolution: Radicals, Resisters, Vets, Hippies, and the Year America Lost Its Mind and Found Its Soul*. New York: Random House, 2016.

Carter, Stephen. *The Violence of Peace: America's Wars in the Age of Obama*. Philadelphia, PA: Beast Books with Perseus Books Group, 2011.

Chomsky, Noam. *Who Rules the World*, New York: Metropolitan Books, 2016

Churchill, Ward, and Jim Vander Wall. *The COINTELPRO Papers: Documents from the FBI's Secret Wars Against Domestic Dissent*. Boston: South End, 1990.

Coffin, William Sloan. *Once to Every Man: A Memoir*. New York: Atheneum, 1977.

Cortright, David. *Soldiers in Revolt: The American Military Today*. Garden City, NY: Anchor/Doubleday, 1975.

Dancis, Bruce. *Resister: A Story of Protest and Prison During the Vietnam War*. Ithaca, NY: Cornell University Press, 2014.

DeBenedetti, Charles. *An American Ordeal: The Antiwar Movement of the Vietnam Era.* Syracuse, NY: Syracuse University Press, 1990.

Diamond, Jared. *Collapse: How Societies Choose to Fail or Succeed.* New York: Viking Press, 2005.

Didion, Joan. *Slouching Towards Bethlehem: Essays.* New York: Farrar, Straus & Giroux, 1968.

Duffett, John, ed. *Against the Crime of Silence: Proceedings of the International War Crimes Tribunal.* New York: Clarion, 1970.

Eckstein, Arthur. *Bad Moon Rising: How the Weather Underground Beat the FBI and Lost the Revolution.* New Haven, CT: Yale University Press, 2016.

Ellsberg, Daniel. *Secrets: A Memoir of Vietnam and the Pentagon Papers.* New York: Viking, 1972.

Flynn, George Q. *The Draft: 1940–1973.* Lawrence, KS: University Press of Kansas, 1993.

Flynn, John T. *As We Go Marching.* New York: Doubleday, 1944.

Foley, Michael Stewart. *Confronting the War Machine: Draft Resistance during the Vietnam War.* Chapel Hill, NC: The University of North Carolina Press; New edition, 2003.

Forest, Jim. *The Root of War Is Fear: Thomas Merton's Advice to Peacemakers.* New York: Orbis Books, 2016.

Friedan, Betty. *The Feminine Mystique.* New York: W. W. Norton, 1963.

Gandhi, M. K. *Non-Violent Resistance (Satyagraha).* New York: Shocken Books, 1961.

Gitlin, Todd. *The Sixties: Years of Hope, Days of Rage.* New York: Bantam Books, 1987.

Goldberg, Danny. *In Search of the Lost Chord: 1967 and the Hippie Idea.* New York. Akashic Books, 2017.Ê

Goodman, Paul. *Growing Up Absurd.* New York: Vintage, 1962.

Gottlieb, Sherry Gershon. *Hell No, We Won't Go: Resisting the Draft during the Vietnam War.* New York: Viking, 1991.

Gould, Richard. *Refusal to Submit: Roots of the Vietnam War and a Young Man's Draft Resistance.* Denver, CO: Susan Kaplan, 2017.

Greer, Germaine. *The Female Eunuch.* New York: McGraw-Hill, 1971.

Hagedorn, Ann. *The Invisible Soldiers: How America Outsourced Our Security.* New York: Simon & Schuster, 2014.

Halberstam, David. *The Best and The Brightest.* New York: Random House, 1972.

Hall, Mitchell K., ed. *Opposition to War: An Encyclopedia of U. S. Peace and Anti war Movements* [2 volumes]. Santa Barbara, CA: ABC-CLIO, 2018.

Hanh, Trich Nhat. *Creating True Peace: Ending Violence in Yourself, Your Family, Your Community, and the World.* New York: Free Press, 2003.

Harris, David. *I Shoulda Been Home Yesterday.* New York: Delacorte, 1976.

Hayden, Tom. *Hell No: The Forgotten Power of the Vietnam Peace Movement.* New Haven, CT: Yale University Press, 2017.

Heller, Joseph. *Catch-22.* New York: Simon & Schuster, 1961.

Herr, Michael. *Dispatches.* New York: Alfred A. Knopf, 1977.

Hopkins, Mary R., ed. *Men of Peace: World War II Conscientious Objectors.* Caye Caulker, Belize: Producciones de la Hamaca, 2009.

Huxley, Aldous. *The Doors of Perception.* New York: Harper and Brothers, 1954.

Kaiser, David. *An American Tragedy: Kennedy, Johnson, and the Origin of the Vietnam War.* Cambridge, MA: Harvard University Press, 2000.

King, Martin Luther Jr. *Where Do We Go from Here: Chaos or Community?* Boston: Beacon Press; Reprint edition, 2010.

Krassner, Paul. *How a Satirical Editor Became a Yippie Conspirator in Ten Easy Years.* New York: Putnam, 1971.

Kunen, James Simon. *The Strawberry Statement: Notes of a College Revolutionary.* New York: Random House, 1969.

Lewes, James. *Protest and Survive: Underground GI Newspapers During the Vietnam War.* Santa Barbara, CA: Praeger, 2003.

Lynd, Alice and Staughton Lynd. *Moral Injury and Nonviolent Resistance: Breaking the Cycle of Violence in the Military and Behind Bars.* Oakland, CA: PM Press, 2017.

Lynd, Staughton, and Michael Ferber. *The Resistance.* Boston: Beacon, 1970.

Mailer, Norman. *The Armies of the Night.* New York: New American Library, 1968.

—*Why Are We in Vietnam? A Novel.* New York: G. P. Putnam, 1967.

Malcolm X, with Alex Haley. *The Autobiography of Malcolm X.* New York: Grove Press, 1965.

Maranis, David. *They Marched into Sunlight: War and Peace Vietnam and America October 1967.* New York: Simon & Schuster, 2003.

Masters, Carol, and Marv Davidov. *You Can't Do That: Marv Davidov, Nonviolent Revolutionary.* Minneapolis, MN: Nodin Press, 2009.

McHenry, Keith with Chaz Bufe. *The Anarchist Cookbook.* Tucson, AZ: See Sharp Press, 2015

Morrison, Joan, and Robert K. Morrison, eds. *From Camelot to Kent State: The Sixties Experience in the Words of Those Who Lived It.* New York: Times Books, 1987.

Nagler, Michael N. *The Nonviolence Handbook: A Guide for Practical Action.* San Francisco, CA: Berrett-Koehler Publishers, Inc., 2014.

New York Times, The. *The Pentagon Papers.* New York: Quadrangle Books, 1971.

Nguyen, Viet Thanh. *Nothing Ever Dies: Vietnam and the Memory of War.* Cambridge, MA: Harvard University Press, 2016.

Remnick, David. *King of the World: Muhammad Ali and the Rise of an American Hero.* New York: Random House, 1998.

Roszak, Theodore. *The Making of a Counterculture: Reflections on the Technocratic Society and Its Youthful Opposition.* New York: Anchor Books/Doubleday, 1969.

Ryan, R. M. *There's a Man with a Gun Over There.* Sag Harbor, NY: The Permanent Press, 2015.

Sanders, Edward. *1968: A History in Verse.* Santa Rosa, CA: Black Sparrow Press, 1997.

Sharp, Gene. *Waging Nonviolent Struggle: 20th Century Practice and 21st Century Potential.* Manchester, NH: Extending Horizons Books, 2005.

Sheehan, Neil. *A Bright Shining Lie: John Paul Vann and America in Vietnam.* New York: Random House, 1988.

Shock, Kurt. *Civil Resistance Today.* Malden, MA: Polity Press, 2015.

Sibley, Mulford Q. *Pacifism, Socialism, Anarchism: which way to peace and justice?* New York: War Resisters League, 1980.

Skolnick, Jerome. *The Politics of Protest.* New York: Ballantine Books, 1967.

Small, Melvin, and William D. Hoover. *Give Peace a Chance: Exploring the Vietnam Antiwar Movement.* Syracuse, NY: Syracuse University Press, 1992.

Sontag, Susan. *Trip to Hanoi.* New York: Farrar, Straus & Giroux, 1968.

Swanson, David. *War Is a Lie.* Charlottesville, VA: Just World Books, 2nd edition, 2016.

Taylor, Telford. *Nuremburg and Vietnam.* Chicago: Quadrangle Books, 1970.

Thorpe, Rebecca. *The American Warfare State: The Domestic Politics of Military Spending.* Chicago: The University of Chicago Press, 2014.

Tilsen, Kenneth E. *Judging the Judges: Justice, Punishment, Resistance, and the Minnesota Court During the War in Vietnam.* St. Cloud, MN: North Star Press of St. Cloud, Inc., 2002.

Trumbo, Dalton. *Johnny Got His Gun.* Philadelphia, PA: J. B. Lippincott, 1939.

Truong, Nhu Tang, with David Chanoff and Doan Van Taoi. *A Viet Cong Memoir: An Inside Account of the Vietnam War and Its Aftermath.* New York: Harcourt Brace Jovanovich, 1985.

Tuchman, Barbara W. *The March of Folly: From Troy to Vietnam.* New York: Alfred A. Knopf, 1984.

Vinen, Richard. *1968: Radical Protest and Its Enemies.* New York: Harper, 2018.

Vonnegut, Kurt. *Slaughterhouse Five.* New York: Delacorte, 1969.

Walburn, Roberta. *Miles Lord: The Maverick Judge Who Brought Corporate America to Justice.* Minneapolis, MN: University of Minnesota Press, 2017.

Wells, Tom. *The War Within: America's Battle over Vietnam.* Oakland, CA: University of California Press, 1994.

Wolfe, Tom. *The Electric Kool-Aid Acid Test.* New York: Farrar, Straus & Giroux, 1968.

Zaroulis, Nancy, and Gerald Sullivan. *Who Spoke Up: American Protest Against the War in Vietnam, 1963–1972.* Garden City, NY: Doubleday, 1984.

Zimmerman, Bill. *Troublemaker: A Memoir from the Front Lines of the Sixties.* New York: Doubleday, 2011.

Zinn, Howard. *A People's History of the United States.* New York: Harper & Row, 1980.

Zirin, David. *What' My Name, Fool? Sports and Resistance in the United States.* Chicago: Haymarket Books, 2005.

INDEX

ACKNOWLEDGMENTS

Who writes any book, even a memoir, in isolation? I know I would not have brought this project to completion without the help, encouragement, and support of many people. Nor could I have lived the life depicted without the involvement of the movement people who lived and loved and worked to end the war and the draft. I will forever hold them all in my heart, even if I have inadvertently missed some of their names in this list.

First of all, I must credit Gini Holland and Noah Tabakin for their inspiration, encouragement, editorial advice, support, and their incredible ability to make me laugh. Laughter has been the essential ingredient of our lives together. Paul Caster stands for dedication to craft and vision. Dave Gutknecht was assigned the role of Mentor by me, as was Alex (Sandy) Wilkinson, by virtue of their knowledge, understanding, patience, compassion, and wit. Dave provided food, shelter, memories, editorial support, and high times during the research phase, and Alex also contributed invaluable editorial advice and memory validation. Mark Sachner and MaryLee Knowlton served as grammar mavens. I am much obliged to Paul Lacques for an early read with commentary. No thank you or acknowledgment would even be possible without the support of Chaz Bufe, publisher at See Sharp Press, whose editorial expertise and encouragement have made this book a reality.

I owe a special thank you to the Quaker Friends Meeting of Minneapolis.

Thanks are due to the many librarians and staff members of the many agencies that helped me find and/or figure out so many links to the past, especially The Swarthmore College Peace Collection, The Minnesota Historical Society, The Minnesota Daily Archives, Kaleidoscope (Milwaukee), The Wisconsin Historical Society, The Houston County Historical Society, The Winona County Historical Society, The Milwaukee Public Library, The Minneapolis Public Library, The John F. Kennedy Presidential Library and Museum, The University of Wisconsin-Milwaukee Libraries Digital Collections and Initiatives, Laurie Scheer and the faculty and staff at The

Writers' Institute of the University of Wisconsin—Madison's Division of Continuing Studies, and The Reference Services Branch of the Electronic Records Division of the National Archives and Records Administration, and Matt Olson for web design.

Following are the names of the people I know supported the Resistance in Minnesota during the Sixties. It is by no means a complete list, but it represents my best efforts to remember and identify all those involved. If I have missed anyone who belongs here, I apologize:

Scott Alarik, Chester Anderson, Marty Anderson, Paul Anderson, Brad Beneke, Jim Beck, Mary Berg, Al Bigot, Rick Blake, Robert Bly, Barry Bondhus, Jim Bruggeman, Chester Bruvold, Sally Buckley, Ann Buttrick, John Buttrick, John Caddy, Eddie Callahan, John Cann, John Carroll, Sue Chamberlain, David Christofferson, Charlie Christianson, Karen Clark, Rick Cockerill, Carlotta Collette, Brian Coyle, Robert Creeley, Bert Crocker, George Crocker, John Crocker, Bob Danielson, Marv Davidov, Charles Dingman, David Doi, Dede Doi, Jim Dombrouski, Jim Dunn, Richard Dworkin, Paul Eaves, Mary Edlund, Daniel Ellsberg, Peggy Fagerlie, Sally Fagerlie, Sue Fashant, Ed Felien, John Filter, Rebecca Finch, Lynne Fischer, David Fisher, Mary Pat Flandrick, Lea Foushee, Don Francis, Joan Francis, Carol Gaines, Chris George, James Gibson, Bob Gilliam, Betsy Gilman, Arnie Goldman, Jack Graham, Deidre Graydon, Keith Gunderson, Dave Gutknecht, Doug Gutknecht, Mary Gutknecht, Ronelda Gutknecht, Ruth Ann Gutknecht, John Gutterman, Camilla Hall, Warren Hanson, Tony Hauser, Judy Heimel, Harold Henderson, Sandy Henderson, Maury Hoch, Alan Hooper, William Hunt, Liz Ihrig, Fr. Al Janicke, John Janikowski, Mark Jasenko, Jeff Johnson, Alan Jones, Jan Juntunen, Garrison Keillor, Galway Kinnel, Tom Koberstein, Frank Kronke, Stephanie L'Heureux, Mark Larson, Bob Lehman, Nancy Lehman, Brad Lennon, Larry Leventhal, Peter Lindberg, David Loy, David Luce, John Marnach, Andrea Marvy, Doug Marvy, Michael Meeks, Barbara Metz, Judy Meyers, Dan Miler, Sue Miler, Jeff Miller, Greg Mills, Lucille Moses, Gordon Neilson, Fred Ojile, Don Olson, John Ostfield, David Pence, Ellen Pence, Leah Peterson, Nancy Peterson, Seth Peterson, Rosemary Pierce, Charles Pilsbury, Roberta Plant, Ed Plaster, Susie Plaster, Bart Quale, Carl Rakosi, Gordon Raup, Dale Rawson, Nancy Rehm, Dennis Richter, Martha Roth, Marty Roth, Bruce Rubenstein, David Rubenstein, Marvin Rubin, Leah Rutchick, Vern Rutsala, Fr. Phillip Salem, John Samborski, Ed Sanders, Scott Sandvick, John Sherman, Fran Shor, Mulford Q. Sibley, Pete Simmons, Rick Sklader, Tom Smit, Paul Smith, Kiki Sonnen, Ray St. Louis, Evan Stark,

Ellen Steinmetz, Mary Stewart, Mark Suchy, Romeyn Taylor, Mike Therriault, Peg Thompson, Paul Tidmarsh, Mike Tiger, Dan Tilsen, David Tilsen, Ken Tilsen, Mark Tilsen, Bill Tilton, Chuck Turchick, Tom Utne, Steve Van Drake, Diane Wakoski, Sydney Walter, Jim Welander, Peter Weller, Brian Wells, Paul Wellstone, Gordie Wiegrefe, Alex (Sandy) Wilkinson, Ralph Witcoff, Dave Wood, Doug Woolridge, Joe Wroblewski, Ed Wujciak.